THE SIMPLE
PLEASURES

PIONEER BOOKS

ANDREWS AND McMEEL

A Universal Press Syndicate Company

Kansas City

Pioneer Books are published for the St. Paul Pioneer Press by Andrews and McMeel. Additional copies may be ordered by calling (800) 642-6480.

Library of Congress Cataloging-in-Publication Data

The simple pleasures / [editor, Daniel Kelly].
        p.   cm.
    Collection of simple pleasures reported by
   the readers of the St. Paul Pioneer Press
     ISBN 0-8362-8083-0 : $6.95
    1. Anecdotes. 2. Pleasure. I. Kelly, Daniel
   II. St. Paul Pioneer Press (Saint Paul, Minn : 1909)
   PN6261.S48   1994   94–19755
   081—dc20   CIP

Editor: Daniel Kelly
Editorial Director: David A. Fryxell
Promotion Director: Chris Oshikata
Design Director: Ellen Simonson
Cover Design: Ellen Simonson

CONTENTS

FOREWORD

In August of 1992, a young lady named Brooke called the Bulletin Board Hot Line to say: "Today my friend and I were talking about simple pleasures, and I realized that one of the simplest pleasures and most wonderful things is the sound of rain when you're going to bed. It's just so comforting to hear the rain go pitter-patter against the window."

Since that day, it has been our great pleasure—virtually always simple—to hear of the Simple Pleasures experienced by thousands of Bulletin Board's readers in Minnesota and Wisconsin. I selected about a hundred of them for a chapter in *The Best of Bulletin Board*, published earlier this year by Andrews and McMeel—but those made scarcely a dent in the inventory.

In this volume, you'll find many, many more—pleasures of many sorts, in which I hope you'll find pleasures of your own.

Daniel Kelly

SIMPLE PLEASURES OF
The Senses

Gramma Judie of Stillwater: "This fall, driving through the countryside early in the morning, I witnessed the beauty of hundreds of intricate spiderwebs hanging over the landscape, fences, signs and any other objects in their paths. It was a foggy morning, but the webs glistening in the light of day told of many hours of diligent work. It was an awesome sight indeed!"

Snowbal of Inver Grove Heights, while putting on her costume for a dance recital: "It has all these sequins on it, and they hit the light, and it makes all these little dots and rainbows bounce off the wall. That's my simple pleasure."

Carol of St. Paul: "I have a lamp with prisms, and when the sun is just right, my whole room is filled with rainbows—all over the floor, the walls and the ceiling. It's just mesmerizing."

Morgan of St. Paul: "My simple pleasure occurs perhaps twice a year, when the sun hits just the right angle. I awake to the sun rays over the bed and watch as dust motes do a slow 3-D gavotte just above my eyes. This has always fascinated me;

some move up, some down, for reasons of probably simple physics as yet unexplained to me at least, yet with grace Nijinsky would envy and subtlety at which Balanchine or da Vinci would marvel."

Turtle of St. Paul: "I just got contacts, and my simple pleasure is getting them in on the first try."

Lori of Woodbury: "I'm a waitress, and I wear contacts—so my great pleasure is to take those contacts off after wearing them in that smoky, greasy environment all day."

Bill of Oakdale: "A simple pleasure I discovered today: when you get a new prescription for your glasses, and you first put them on, and suddenly you can see clearly. I look around the room, and I can read things that are normally blurry."

A.J. of Eau Claire, Wis.: "I have two really close friends who are blind, and every time I find myself describing something I think is beautiful, I realize how really lucky I am to be sighted. That goes for hearing . . . and all the other senses."

Joybubbles of Minneapolis, who is blind: "One of life's distinctive pleasures is door-bumper twanging.

"You know, behind a lot of doors, there are these round, long, skinny things—about the size of a crayon, I guess—with a rubber tip at the end, and the door bumps against those instead of the wall. If you go behind the door and get down on the floor, like this, and reach out and grab this thing and flick it like this [*ba-boing, ba-boing, ba-boing*], it makes the prettiest little sound [*ba-boing*].

"Door-bumper twanging—I recommend it. And if you don't like to sit down, you can always do it with your feet. You can mount 'em any convenient place for twanging. Get as many as you want. Well, good-bye—and [*ba-boing*] to ya."

Sergeant Bilko of St. Paul: "Outside my office window, I hear a cardinal chirping. I can't see her, but I know her distinctive voice. It's nice to have a touch of the natural world whilst stuck at work."

John of St. Paul: "I live over here by Como Park—and there's a guy who plays bagpipes out in the park. It's absolutely wonderful to walk out on a fall day and hear the sound of pipes being played."

J.N. of North St. Paul: "On beautiful days when the temperature's just right, I sit on my back porch with the windows open and play Dvořák on my cello. I forget about the conflicts and dilemmas of the world, and enjoy the birds singing their own karaoke accompaniment. I pretend Dvořák wrote the part that the birds sing, because he took all his melodies from nature.

"Then I hear another melody: children asking for snacks. I know Dvořák didn't write this one; he had a wife and a housemaid. Back to reality for me."

Patti of River Falls, Wis.: "One of my simplest pleasures is finishing every bit of housework and sitting back on the couch in complete silence, to enjoy the sound of clean."

Dud: "I opened a can of Campbell's Cream of Mushroom soup, and it slid right out in a perfect can-shaped chunk and splatted in the pan. It works with Cream of Chicken—and Tomato, too. I just love it when that happens."

Wubba of South St. Paul: "The sound when you shake out the SPAM from its can—that suckling kind of sound? It just completely affirms that you're eating something worthwhile. It's just a beautiful thing."

Jim Clark of White Bear Lake: "I've got two boys, and I can identify each of them by the clunking that they make comin' down the stairs, and the shuffling across the living room, and the scraping of their chairs at the kitchen table, and their flopping on the beanbag. It would be such a heartache if I didn't hear that clunkin' and shufflin' and scrapin' and floppin'."

Guinevere of Afton: "What I've just realized is a simple pleasure: when I hear some sort of emergency vehicle off in the distance—a fire truck or a police siren or an ambulance siren—and I realize that all my family is accounted for, and I don't have to worry about them."

Louise of St. Paul: "I just helped my two grandsons put a Lego system together. It's a simple pleasure to hear the final pieces snap together."

Danno of Burnsville: "I have nine brothers and sisters, and when we were growing up, we had a three-bedroom house—so sleeping spaces were at a premium. One of the premium places was our three-season porch, which had a tin roof.

"To hear the sound of rain hitting a tin roof—it's the most peaceful, tranquil, hypnotizing sound you can imagine. And to this day, I still miss that sound."

Arlene of St. Paul: "When I was a kid, I loved the sound of the old trains. I had my husband buy me a choo-choo train engine that runs around on the floor and toots and smokes and everything. I've even taped movies that have old choo-choo trains in the background, and I just listen to 'em over and over. I may sound crazy, but it sure is comforting to me."

Julie of Eagan: "My husband and I own 40 acres of land up in northern Wisconsin. My simple pleasure is to be able to walk out into the middle of the woods and hear the peace and quiet.

Simple Pleasures of the Senses   5

No planes, no trains, no cars, no sirens wailing—just peace and quiet, the sounds of the trees and the leaves rustling around your feet. Our first child is gonna be born the first of January, and I'm very glad that I'll be able to pass this on."

Pete Peterson of Osceola, Wis.: "We live in the country—and in western Wisconsin, that means dairy farms. In the spring and the fall, when it's cold enough so that our farmer neighbors are heating with wood but warm enough to keep the cows' manure from freezing, the smells of wood smoke and fresh manure mingle to form an aroma that is a harbinger of the change of seasons to come. It's particularly pleasant in the early morning, when the air is calm, and it's even more enjoyable when a passing flock of geese or a strutting pheasant rooster add their morning sounds to the mixture."

Anonymous man: "I just loved it the other day, when the breeze was comin' out of the southwest over the woods, bringin' the smell of the woods into where I work. That's the most beautiful smell in the world: the smell of the forest. Can't beat it. No way."

Linda of Hugo: "A warm summer night when an unexpected breeze brings the sweet scent of purple petunias into the living room."

Calamity of St. Paul: "A barn full of new-mown hay: There's nothing better-smelling than that. Or if you just open a coffee can—that first little gasp of air? Ohhh, coffee smells so good."

Shirley of Marine: "I stopped at the grocery store today on the way home from work, and I bought some fresh-ground coffee. It smells so good that I took the long way home."

Gretchen of Shoreview: "My simple pleasure is when I wake up—and that's early; 5 A.M.—and my roommates, who don't drink coffee, have already started my coffee for me. I can smell it when I walk up the stairs. It's the most pleasant smell to wake up to. And my roommates' simple pleasure is smelling me in the morning when I get out of the shower, because I smell so good."

Roger Smith of St. Paul: "The old lady's making homemade bread, and you sit back and watch TV—and the smell of it is just wild. Best pleasure there ever was: homemade bread—"

BULLETIN BOARD NOTES: *At which point we heard boisterous female laughter in the background. The old lady, no doubt.*

AnnMarie of Rochester: "I walk my dog every day around 5:30 P.M., in our neighborhood—and my pleasure is when I can smell what people are preparing for dinner."

Anna of St. Paul (whose lungs would appear to be world-class): "My simple pleasure is when you're walking down the street in the winter with your friend, and then you see this smoke coming out of a house, and you stop, and it's this cool smell of somebody drying their clothes, and it's just a really cool smell, and my friend is sitting here laughing at me, but it's just a cool simple pleasure, OK? And I hope you put this in the paper, because this is costing me a quarter, because I'm calling from Snyder's. OK, bye." (Anna called again, immediately thereafter: "The phone is, like, messed up or something, and it gave me my quarter back, and I thought that was really cool, so I'm using the same quarter to call you twice! You should feel really privileged. OK, bye.")

Warner of Osceola, Wis.: "When I was younger and it was a hot day out, I would go down in the basement and I would open our big freezer up and kinda stick half of my body in there—and it felt good! Cooled me off!

"Well, by and by, the more I did it, the more I liked the smell of the freezer—so, some days, just on a whim, nothin' better to do, I'd go down and . . . I guess you'd call it 'smelling my freezer.' That's pretty weird, I guess."

BULLETIN BOARD REPLIES: *Good guess. But nothing to be ashamed of.*

Jim the Hog-ridin' Fool of Stillwater: "I love Harley Davidsons. I love anything with a motor. And the smell that just gets me goin': two-stroke oil. Snowmobiles, outboard motors, anything that's two-stroke—if it's got oil in there and the thing's runnin', boy, I'm just set. Two strokes. I don't know what it is. Ever since I was a little kid."

Kris Valley of Roseville: "Every night, I look forward to coming in to bed and to taking a big whiff of my pillow. That makes me fall asleep right away."

Julie of Cottage Grove: "When I wake up for one of my numerous middle-of-the-night feedings with my newborn, I can smell her daddy's cologne on her blanket and on her PJs from when he held her earlier in the day. Kinda makes me think he's there with me.

"Of course, a better simple pleasure will be when I get to sleep for more than three hours at a time."

Arlene of the East Side: "Snuggling with my little girl after she's had a bath; her clean hair smells heavenly."

Courtney of Woodbury: "The smell of new crayons."

Katie Too: "Puppy breath."

Pat of St. Paul: "The day after Halloween, my son shared with me one of his life's simple pleasures—and that was to open his trick-or-treat bag and take a deep whiff of all that aroma."

N.C. of Eau Claire, Wis.: "We have a cupboard for just spices and herbs, and every time I open the door, the aroma of all those wonderful spices and herbs mingled together makes me smile. It's earthy and exotic and homey all at once."

Debbie of parts undisclosed: "We were going down to the farmers' market in downtown St. Paul. We were a block away, and we could smell the dill in the air. I thought: There's a simple pleasure for you."

Beanbag of parts hereabouts: "I have a nephew who loves to can dill pickles. He loves the smell of dill so much that he'll pack a whole bouquet of fresh dill and keep it in the back of his van, so he can smell it all the time he's in his van."

Axman of Mondovi, Wis.: "A simple woodcutting pleasure: the smell of white oak when the saw bites into it. It's the same as bourbon, and for good reason: Bourbon takes its aroma from the white oak barrels it's aged in."

Connie of River Falls, Wis.: "My honey and I were doing a woodworking project last weekend, and the simple pleasure that we both noticed is: cutting with a power saw through nice pine boards, and the scent of the pine really gets strong."

Ice of Eau Claire, Wis., a firefighter: "When we work downtown, at Station 2, we have a huge popcorn machine—and after we get done fighting a fire, and everyone's tuckered out, and there's the smell of smoke running through the station, we get upstairs and put on a fresh batch of popcorn, and it's just the greatest smell in the world."

BULLETIN BOARD MUSES: *Unless, of course, some fool burns it.*

Cee Dee of Highland Park: "You know how you get a popcorn hull stuck in your teeth, and you get it out with a toothpick? You finally get it out, and it feels so good, 'cause it's been buggin' you for so long."

Joe of Minneapolis: "Corn-on-the-cob—when the ears have exactly 16 rows of kernels so I can eat four rows at a time and have them come out even. Fourteen or 18 rows leaves two left over. And 12 rows of kernels is not suitable because you have to cut at too deep of an angle and you get a little bit of cob when you bite."

Tim H. of St. Paul: "I'm so proud of myself; I just had to call and tell someone.

"On Sunday morning, I like fried eggs for breakfast. For the first time in four years, I got all three eggs in the pan and flipped without breaking one yolk. Now, I realize that for many culinary experts, this is no big deal. But I always end up breaking one or two yolks—so if this isn't a simple pleasure, I don't know what is. I'm gonna have a great day today; I can feel it."

Lolly of West St. Paul: "We get bacon about once, twice a year, and my absolute most decadent pleasure is eating eggs that have been fried in that bacon fat. I can just feel my coronary arteries curdling, or corroding. It's the most delicious pleasure."

Starboard of Oakdale: "My simple pleasure is being able to sit through a whole lunch without any of my friends telling me how many grams of fat are in each little bite or morsel of food I take, how many calories, how much sodium, how much . . . everything, in everything I eat."

Art Thell of West St. Paul: "When I was a teenager on the farm at Freeport, it was not unusual to do late-fall field work such as plowing or disking after coming home from school. I would work until 10 or so, taking along sandwiches and coffee. The air would usually have a nasty bite to it up on that John Deere, but those sandwiches had a taste all their own, made of homemade bread and toasted over the tractor manifold."

Sweet William of Shoreview: "The first bacon, lettuce and tomato sandwich of the season—when the home-grown beef-steak tomatoes come in."

Apple Annie of St. Paul: "One of my favorite things to eat when fall rolls around and winter sets in is a hot, steaming dish of oatmeal. Add a dash of cinnamon; a cut-up, fresh, juicy apple; and toss in a few walnuts or pecans. It's old-fashioned goodness in a modern world."

Jeanne of St. Paul: "When I finish a box of cornflakes and there's not enough in that box and I have to open a new box. There's nothing nicer than a new box of cornflakes—with the big flakes and all the crunchiness."

Laura of "really far away": "I just got home after being away for three weeks, and there was a bag of tortilla chips on top of my microwave. I opened it up, and they were still fresh and still crunchy. I was so happy."

Linda of Oakdale: "Eating the little crunchy batter at the bottom of a corn dog."

Nipper of White Bear Lake: "Scraping just enough peanut butter out of the jar for one more sandwich. I love that."

T.O. of River Falls, Wis.: "This time of the year, we munch upon salted-in-the-shell peanuts and throw the empty shells back into the bowl of whole ones. My simple pleasure is, after everyone else has abandoned the bowl of shells, digging around and finding that 'one more' unopened peanut—sometimes after you *know* you've found them all."

Corey Peterson of La Crosse, Wis.: "Opening a bag of pistachios, eating them out of the shells, taking your hand in there and finding one pistachio covered with salt, already out of the shell."

J.B. of Afton: "After finishing a large fries from McDonald's, reaching into the bag and realizing that there's still a handful left at the bottom."

The Old Curmudgeon of Lino Lakes: "I was wounded on Okinawa, and I got on a hospital ship—and what did they serve us but boiled potatoes. Not dehydrated; not anything false. Real, honest-to-god boiled murphies. I don't recall that I even put salt on them. They were so good, just plain."

Mommy of White Bear Lake: "Virgin mashed potatoes. You know the kind: They're all white and whipped up, and there's a little pool of butter in the middle, and no one's touched them yet."

A.C. of White Bear Lake: "After being out in the winter—chopping wood or shoveling snow—it's great to come in to a lunch of hot tomato soup and grilled cheese sandwiches. You have to put chunks of cheddar cheese in the bottom of the soup, so they melt. It's perfect."

M.S. of St. Paul: "I'm a college student, and my simple pleasure is when I'm hungry for a piece of cheese, and I go to the refrigerator to get a piece of cheese—and it's not moldy. It's the greatest thing. And then, if I want to put the cheese in a sandwich—and the bread's not moldy, either! It's just great."

Mark of Woodbury: "A loaf of bread with no holes in it, so the jelly doesn't drip through."

Phyllis Warden of Rochester: "Freshly baked chocolate-chip cookies and a very cold glass of milk."

C.J. of Eagan: "After eating Cocoa Krispies: all the chocolate milk you get to drink that the Cocoa Krispies made."

Michelle of St. Paul: "When you're drinking either a cold glass of Kool Aid or a warm glass of hot cocoa, you can feel it going all the way down to your stomach. It's just . . . invigorating."

Nia of Roseville: "I'm sitting here doing my homework and drinking a cup of cocoa. My simple pleasure is finishing the cup of cocoa and getting that cocoa sludge at the bottom of my cup, and having to eat that up with a spoon."

St. Pauli Girl No. 2: "When I was a kid, we were never allowed to have sugared cereal. My mom was a North Dakota farm girl who grew up during the Depression, so sugared cereal was considered frivolous as well as non-nutritious. As if that wasn't bad enough, she never purchased real milk from the store. We had to make it using powdered milk. Yuck. Come to think of it, I didn't host many sleep-overs as a kid. My friends must have known what fate awaited them at breakfast time. Sadly, my young social life was thwarted by instant milk.

"My simple pleasure is sitting down to a big bowl of Cap'n Crunch with store-bought milk poured all over it."

Young Kelly of Woodbury: "My simple pleasure is putting sugar on your Rice Krispies, and it all sinks to the bottom, and then when you're all done and you go to drink the milk, you get a big mouthful of sugar and it crunches in your mouth. You guys should try it sometime."

BULLETIN BOARD REPLIES: *We have tried it . . . or, should we say, did try it—many, many times, until we got it just right. Check our dental records sometime.*

Carol of Eagan: "I work in St. Paul as a dental hygienist—and I love to eat Blow Pops comin' home from work. Eatin' all that sugar and chewin' that gum—it's just what I need after spendin' a day in someone's mouth."

Tim of South St. Paul: "I recently had my wisdom teeth pulled, and the simple pleasure I have is just eatin' lunch or dinner or whatever and then usin' this little syringe and rinsin' out my sockets and watchin' all this food come out. I know it's gross, but it's somethin' you should all try at least once. It's kinda cool."

Joel of Redwood Falls: "This is kinda cool for me: putting about 15 or 20 grapes in your mouth all at one time—preferably red grapes—and just biting down and chewing them, feeling all the juice just squirt around in your mouth."

Millie of St. Paul: "Popping little cherry tomatoes in my mouth, biting down and letting the juice squirt all over inside my mouth."

Mike on the Bluff: "One of my great pleasures is eating fresh raspberries that I get from my granddaughter Michelle, whose simple pleasure is to pick them. She picks them and then brings them over to me. Ain't that sweet?"

Kathy of Roseville: "When you make a can of orange juice and you pull off that white strip, then lift off the top, don't you just love to lick that drop off the bottom there? It's real sweet and juicy."

Bernie of Burnsville: "A simple pleasure: buying ice cream at the grocery store, and by the time I get home, it has gotten soft at the top of the carton. I eat all the softened ice cream immediately. The ice cream in that carton never tastes that good again."

Joe of Brooklyn Park: "I just got done eatin' these super-spicy chicken wings, and I love it when my head itches and I start sweatin' off them darn little things."

Jennifer of St. Paul: "My simple pleasure is the belch I have after having gorged myself with pizza."

M.C. of South St. Paul: "I have a simple pleasure: about an hour after I wake up in the morning, that stretch—that first stretch, where everything cracks and pops. Ohhh-aaaaahhhhh. Nothin' like it."

Jennifer of South St. Paul: "Cracking my toes. I live for it."

Max of Mendota Heights: "The basement floor is ice-cold. You're looking for something in the laundry. Your feet are freezing. You find a pair of socks that have been in the dryer. They're warm. You put 'em on your feet, and your body is warm all over. That is a wonderful simple pleasure."

Brad of Little Canada: "There's no feelin' in the world like puttin' on a brand-new pair of socks, right out of the package. When I get rich, I'm gonna wear a brand-new pair of socks every day for the rest of my life."

Inez of the West Side: "My simple pleasure is to get into a bathtub, take a real soapy washrag and wash my feet. It doesn't get much better than that."

Wayne of Hastings: "Putting my feet in the bathtub when my kids are taking a bath and having them pour warm water over my legs."

Laurie of Maplewood: "Taking a hot, hot bath and sticking

my toe up into the faucet and having icy-cold water drip on my feet. It's great."

JB's Wife: "The other night, JB and I were discussing how we spent that day, and he mentioned that one of the best parts was when he took a long, relaxing bath. It felt so good to totally unwind and scratch his back with the back-scratching brush. He said he should relax like that more often . . . a warm bath and a good back scratch.

"I asked him what brush he used, and he said the green one hanging from the shower head. I'm afraid I shattered his simple pleasure when I told him we didn't have a back-scratching brush. He had been using the brush I use to scrub the toilet bowl."

Mama Bear of White Bear Lake: "I wear those pantyhose that are supposed to massage your legs all day. Let's face it; they're support hose. Well, those types of pantyhose have a nasty habit of massaging their way *down* your legs; in other words, they tend to sag by midday. Well, my simple pleasure is going into the ladies' room at lunchtime and, starting at the toes, pulling them *all* the way back up again. They feel like I just put them on, in the middle of the day."

Sue of parts undisclosed: "Coming home from work after a long, hard day, taking off my pantyhose that have been cutting into my waist all day, sitting on the toilet and scratching my belly until I think I'm in heaven . . . ahhhhh!!!"

Kathryn of Brooklyn Center: "When I get home from working all day in tight pantyhose, or if I've been running errands in snug jeans, I like to slip on a pair of my old knit maternity pants—even though I gave birth six months ago. They are so loose and wonderfully comfortable; they make me feel skinny."

Reed of western Wisconsin: "I'm usually a satin-and-lace kind of girl, but every once in a while, I have to dig to the bottom of my lingerie drawer and dig out those cotton underwear and bras. It just feels so comforting that you wouldn't believe it."

B.C. of St. Paul (echoed by *Jessie* of Hastings): "When you get a brand-new tube of Chap Stick, and it's the first time you use it, and the top is all nice and smooth. I just love that."

Mary of White Bear Lake: "My simple pleasure: touching and feeling the softness of the inside of my newborn's hand. It was softer than silk, and I would just sit and rub it all the time. It felt so good."

Fiamma of Forest Lake: "Hand lotion on dry, weary, wintered hands."

Josh of Hamline University: "When we lived on our farm in Elk River, we always would go up to our cows and stick our fingers in their mouths. They would just suck and suck—the little calves—because they were thinking that they were sucking on their mothers' teats. That was a good time for me."

The Mom of Six of Hastings: "Three weeks ago, I had surgery on my wrist, and I've had a cast on it. Yesterday, I got the cast off and I was able to stand in the shower with no bread bag wrapped around my arm and wash my hair with both hands. It was a wonderful feeling. For all of you people who go through life one-handed: God bless you. I know what it must be like."

Connie of St. Paul: "You know when you're wearing tennis shoes, or other shoes that have tongues in 'em, and you're walkin' around and your feet are kinda sore, and you look down and the tongue's kinda slid down the side of your foot—and then when you straighten it out, that just feels wonderful."

Barry of Eagan: "I'm a mailman—or a letter carrier, for the PC crowd—with a walking route. My simple pleasure is when I stop for lunch and take my shoes and socks off. Out of my blue-collar briefcase (a.k.a. lunch pail) emerges my frozen water bottle, which I rub all over my aching feet. Oh, what a relief it is! I polish it all off with a heels-up power nap."

Andrew of New Brighton: "A simple pleasure is when you lace your workout shoes real tight, work out for a few hours and your feet are all sore, and then you go home and take your shoes off, and all the blood rushes back into your feet."

Sweaty of North Oaks: "One of life's simplest pleasures is knowing that you've worked out so hard and feeling one bead of sweat drip down your back, right onto your tailbone."

Becca of Mahtomedi: "I'm on the soccer team at my school, and every day after soccer practice, my feet are all wet from running around on the field and chasing after the soccer balls that got stuck in the swamp and stuff. My simple pleasure is to take my shoes and my wet socks and my wet shin pads off and walk through the grass to my car. It's the best feeling in the whole world."

Megan of Roseville: "I have to get ready for my volleyball game, and I forgot to wash my uniform, so it was all sweaty from the last game. I went down to the basement, in the laundry, and my mom had washed it last night, and it was out on the rack—all clean and dry. That is a simple pleasure: a clean uniform for volleyball."

Julie of Gopher Prairie: "One of my favorite simple pleasures is letting my hair down after a long day, when I've had it up in a bun all day, really tight."

ShadowCat of Rosemount: "My favorite simple pleasure is

when my husband brushes my long hair for me. He brushes, and brushes, and brushes—with a natural-bristle brush, of course. It just makes me purr."

Kate of Eagan, liberally punctuated with the giggles: "Last night, I'm sittin' here alone; it's Friday night, and I figured: This would be a good time to shave! So I got out the cool menthol Barbasol, and I shaved my armpits. So I finished taking my shower, and then I was done—and I felt a little tingling in my armpits. The cool menthol was causing that little tingle, and it was really, really lovely. I've shared way too much; I'll call you back later."

Free to Be Hair-free of St. Paul: "My simple pleasure is shaving my legs after letting the hair grow for three weeks, and then rolling around in bed and feeling the sheets rub against them."

Scruffy of Hastings: "My boyfriend and his brother are on a weeklong motorcycle trip to some race in Ohio. My simple pleasure is not shaving my legs the entire time he's gone.

"My hair grows really fast, so I usually shave every day because I don't want him to feel any pricklies when we're snuggling. I'm wearing dark hose, so my clients are none the wiser.

"Only the baby and the cats know for sure. The baby doesn't care, and the cats are using me as a scratching post."

SIMPLE PLEASURES OF
Cats and Dogs

The Quilter of the Midway: "Last summer, three tiny kittens started sleeping under the bushes in my front yard. I don't know where they came from, but ever since then, they have stayed around my house—and so I started to feed them.

"When it got cold, I tried to encourage them to come in the house, but they're terrified of people and run as soon as I appear. I am now putting out three or four bowls of cat food each day, and by evening, the food is all gone.

"My simple pleasure is: Just after it snows, I see hundreds of tiny footprints leading up to my front door, coming from all directions, and sometimes I see small bundles of fur sitting on my front walk.

"This has also created a simple displeasure: I worry that sometime, one of these little fur balls will come up to my step and find the food dish empty. My wish is that if people leave their cats outside, they would have them neutered, so the cats can't have kittens to be left out to starve and become wild."

G of West St. Paul: "It's snowing outside right now—that light, feathery snow that lets you see each individual flake—and I took my cat outside, with me in my PJs, and just stood there watching the perfect little snowflakes land on his black coat. He thought this was great—and was trying to catch them on the way down."

Randy of Red Wing: "I have two cats, both about three years old. When they start to wrestle—you know, just playfully clawing, scratching, kicking, throwing each other around—it's just great. It's the funniest thing you'll ever see. Professional wrestling has nothing on these two."

Greg of Minneapolis: "I've got two cats—a rather old fellow, and a young four-month-old. The other day, I woke up about two in the morning and looked over next to me, and in the light coming in from the window, the two cats were curled up side-by-side. I mean, it really melted my heart; they're so sweet-lookin' together. Considering that they don't get along much during the day, it's really kind of cool."

Kimberly of Faribault: "I love to watch my two cats clawing on my couch—because I guess they've forgotten that they're both declawed."

Beth of Coon Rapids: "My simple pleasure is holding my

furry, purry cat named Dud and massaging her toes. She loves that, too."

Katie of Maplewood: "I just had a simple pleasure. After you get home from a long day of school, you take off your socks and rub your bare feet on your cat. Feels really good."

Navasanki of St. Paul: "I have a wonderful cat, and I have a terrible job—like most people. I stand on my feet all day, and I come home from work and take off my shoes and socks and put up my feet, and my cat—my wonderful cat—will come up and curl up on my feet. She purrs really loud, and her whole body shakes when she's purrin', so it's like I'm gettin' a nice little foot massage. She sits right on my foot and purrs her little heart out."

Jane of Inver Grove Heights: "My simple pleasure is my cat, Gemini, who recently had to have her front leg amputated due to cancer. At the time, I didn't think she'd be able to do everything that she used to before, but when I first saw her jump on the kitchen table with three legs, that made my day. Now, she does everything she used to before—especially sleep in the middle of my bed so I can't get in."

Debbie of Cottage Grove: "My simple pleasure is when I wake up in the middle of the night, and my cat is sleeping between my legs. It makes you feel really loved."

Rambling Rose of Little Canada: "A simple pleasure: when my kitten comes up to me and snuggles his nose into my neck, and he's purring. He just snuggles and snuggles and snuggles, as if he just can't get close enough to me."

L.A.S. of Inver Grove Heights: "The new scoopable cat litter is the greatest thing. It's almost fun to clean the cat pan."

Diane of the East Side: "One of my simple pleasures is when you have pets, and you get all of those eye boogers out."

Susan of St. Paul: "One of my simple pleasures is lining the puppy kennel of my friend's new puppy—I'm house-sitting now—with pages of the newspaper that I don't particularly want to read, or with stories that really irritate me. That's a simple pleasure: lining the puppy cage with unsavory newspapers."

A.C. of St. Paul: "My simple pleasure is my doggie, Shadow. When I come home after work, she's so excited to see me that she's shaking. She stands up on her back legs and puts her front paws up on my shoulders and tries to kiss me; she shakes, she's so excited to see me.

"And then later on, when we're sitting around relaxing, she crawls up in my lap and turns over on her back and goes to sleep in my lap—which is not an easy thing, because she's a big black Lab."

Barb of St. Paul: "My simple pleasures involve Lucy. She's my puppy. She's a basset hound. I call it the Puppy Head Butt—and that's when she wants me to give her lots of petting, and she comes and bumps into me with her head. Or the Puppy Twist— when she wags her tail so hard that her whole back end and feet twist all the way around."

P.H. Perez of St. Paul: "One of my simple pleasures is looking at the look of appreciation and excitement on my dog's face when we take her out for a walk. She's a big thing; we try to exercise her a lot, but it's never really enough. And when she gets out on the sidewalk and finally realizes that this is for real, this walk, she'll look up and smile the way dogs smile, and she gives this little half-jump and then spears me in the side with her nose. I think it's just great; this animal is eternally grateful just for the fact that I let her out and tie a leash to her neck."

Doug of the East Side: "Our pet recently died—and as much as I loved the critter, it's a real pleasure to be able to put down a plate of food during a commercial to go in and get a drink, and come back and find that the plate's not been knocked on the floor, the food's still on the plate, and there's no animal's face in it."

Mike of Mac-Grove: "I help out with the cooking a lot here at home, especially during the week, and it's nice—when I get going in the kitchen, and sometimes things spill—it's nice to just call the dog over and have the dog eat the stuff up, rather than getting some paper towels and cleaning it up. The dog also works really well in the dining room; we let him in after meals, and he really cleans the place up."

Matt of Oakdale: "My simple pleasure involves shoveling snow when it's nice and light and fluffy—and throwing it at my dog. She can't get enough of it—so if you activists are getting in an uproar, just relax."

Peggy of Roseville: "My simple pleasure is sittin' and singin' to my dog. And don't get me wrong: I'm not a lonely old lady; I have a husband and family that I get a lot of love and affection from. But there's somethin' that's just soothing about sittin' on the floor and puttin' my dog in my arms and lookin' into those big brown eyes and singin'.

"A lot of the stuff I sing to him, I make up. His favorite song is called 'Pussycat Blue, I Love You.'"

Jeanne of Glenwood: "Our old dog, Rudy, has a white muzzle. He's getting slower and spends much of his time snoozing. Sometimes, he'll be laying on the floor on a quiet evening, and I'll hear his tail thumping. When I look up and see him still sleeping, his tail going like he's having a heck of a dream, I feel a surge of affection for him.

"When he's awake, he's sometimes crotchety with the young dog (as are we all). But when he sleeps peacefully and remembers his own youth, he's a good boy."

SIMPLE PLEASURES OF
The Highfalutin Kind

Unfrozen Caveman Accountant of St. Paul: "Last night, at 11:15, I picked up the phone and ordered some new software for my computer from a software place in Seattle. It arrived just as my office opened this morning, at 9 o'clock. In 10 hours, they had pulled my order together, boxed it up and got it to an overnight-delivery company, which got it to me.

"Now, I'm just an unfrozen caveman accountant, so I have no conception of the technology which makes this possible—but I know this much: It's pretty darned impressive."

Debbie of Inver Grove Heights: "We have a computer that's got a 'screen saver'—you know, designs that come and go. We've got one called Dazzle. It comes on in color, and the baby—who's three months old—when he gets kind of fussy, he calms down watching Dazzle on the computer."

The Computer Nerd of Forest Lake: "I've programmed my computers to tell me, every time I turn them on, that they love being my computers."

Simple Pleasures of the Highfalutin Kind   31

Bob Woolley of St. Paul: "There's a great little program called Kaboom that you can add to your home computer, so that instead of making ordinary, boring beeps when some event happens, you can put in other, more interesting sounds. I now have my computer set up so that when I insert a disk, I hear Bart Simpson saying, 'Eat my shorts!' When I eject a disk, I hear Ronald Reagan saying, 'Go ahead, make my day.' And, best of all, when I try to delete something, it warns me, with Ricky Ricardo saying to Lucy, 'Ohhhh, no you dunt.' It just makes the ordinary, mundane work on the computer that much more pleasurable."

Pat of St. Paul: "I was just noticing how much I like the feeling of when you take a videotape cartridge and put it into the VCR. It devours it—kind of sucks it in. And then when you press the Eject button, it kind of coughs it up at you. It's almost like the VCR thing is alive."

Kim Sorensen of Maplewood: "This morning, my 5-year-old daughter asked me what I looked like when I was a baby. I told her that all my baby pictures were in slide form in California at my parents' house, tucked away in a closet collecting dust.

"Then I remembered that my sister made a videotape of all the childhood slides, and she sent me a copy last summer. All I had to do was put the tape in the VCR to enjoy all those baby pictures, while listening to the pretty background music. And I didn't even have to put up a screen or a slide projector. Pure heaven."

Flap Jack of Detroit Lakes: "One of my simple pleasures is using the mute button on the TV remote control. Every time I zap a stupid commercial, I love it, love it, love it."

Neil MacKay of White Bear Lake: "A bonus: I tune out Dan Dierdorf and John Madden when watching football games. I must stay alert and keep busy muting and unmuting, but that's a small price to pay for never hearing their drivel (Dierdorf) or screaming (Madden) again."

Bomber Z. of "Uptown in the big city": "My highfalutin pleasure is those little baby monitors where you can hear the kid cryin' or laughin' or whatever in the other room. My sister-in-law has one that picks up the neighbor's cordless phone. Last night, we were listenin' to her cry on the phone to . . . whoever, 'cause we could only hear one side of it. But she was complainin' and cryin' about how she has a mouse, and describing the little mouse turds in her yard and in the basement. We were wonderin' if she could hear the baby cryin'. It comes in just like you're talkin' to her."

Kelly of Southern Minnesota: "My mom and I and the rest of the congregation were waiting for Mass to begin last Sunday when suddenly this voice came over the speaker system. No one was at the podium or at the altar; no one was anywhere near a microphone. Yet all of us could hear this lady talking and laughing about this bridge party she went to.

"The congregation started giggling, and a man from the parish got up to check out the system. He didn't find anything, so he just returned to his seat for the service.

"It turns out this lady was using a cordless phone whose signal was picked up by the church's microphone system. All I can say is: It's a blessing this lady wasn't calling one of those 976 numbers."

Althea of Vadnais Heights: "I love coming home at the end of the day and finding a whole bunch of blinking lights on my answering machine. It's nice to know that that many people thought about me today—even the one from my husband of 40 years that says: 'Where the hell are you?' It's good to know you're missed."

Mickey of Savage: "One of my life's simple pleasures would have to be when my husband calls and leaves a bitchy message on my answering machine. I like to play it again on fast-forward and hear it sound like the gibberish it is."

Rich of Burnsville: "My highfalutin pleasure involves voice mail: going through a list of messages that have collected while I was out, and being able to delete each one because they're of minor importance—and after the last message, the electronic message tells you: 'You have no messages remaining. Good-bye.'"

Liza and Dana's Mom of Inver Grove Heights: "My highfalutin pleasure is accessing my e-mail account on our family PC and communicating with my daughters, who are attending college in Oklahoma and Iowa. What is really fun is when Liza happens to be in the computer lab at the same time I'm logged onto my account, and one of us requests a 'Chat.' The screen splits in half, with her typing on one half and me on the other. We can have a real conversation electronically!"

Audrey of St. Paul: "For 35 years, we lifted the heavy door on our tuck-under garage. At the age of 65, we gave ourselves a retirement gift: a garage-door opener. Now, we feel pampered when we drive in and out of our home, in all kinds of weather, with the greatest of ease."

Dale of Eau Claire, Wis.: "I have a little box that looks like a garage-door opener, and if we're going the speed limit down the interstate or some other road and one of these idiots comes up behind us at a high rate of speed and just so happens to have a radar detector in his car, a simple blip of the button will set off all radar detectors within about a half-mile. It really gives one a feeling of doing your civic duty."

DeeDee of West St. Paul: "My simple pleasure is using the cruise control in my car. I especially love it after I have to slow down in traffic, and then I can just push that Resume button—and the car just goes right back up to the speed I was at! It is so amazing that someone was smart enough to invent that."

Gene of St. Paul: "I had open-heart surgery a couple of years ago. Ended up with an artificial aortic valve. Had severe complications, and almost died. But now, when I wake up in the morning and I feel that valve working with a strong, slow, steady pulse, I know I'm gonna have another good day. One more day—and that is, for me, a big, big life's pleasure."

Cynthia of West St. Paul: "A week ago today, I received a new heart—and I'm sitting right now in a quiet hospital room watching the monitor go *beep . . . beep . . . beep* with a steady, even rhythm, which my heart hasn't done in years, and knowing that somebody's gift has made it possible for me to look forward to a healthy future with my kids.

"Some simple pleasures aren't simple at all; they're very complex, and very treasured."

SIMPLE PLEASURES OF
Christmas

Wheelin' Willie of West St. Paul: "As I was biking over to a friend's house, I stopped by a nearby lake and wrote MERRY CHRISTMAS across it in 15-, 20-foot letters, only to be seen from the sky.

"I hope somebody will fly over in the next few days and check it out, 'cause I sure had a gas writin' it."

Kathy of St. Paul: "A simple pleasure: It's on Christmas Eve, when you're watching the news on TV or listening to the radio, and all of a sudden they'll stop and say: 'Oh, we have this news bulletin! The radar has seen an unidentified flying object that appears to be a small sleigh and eight tiny reindeer'—and you have all of these adults, with straight faces, carrying on with this news story.

"I remember hearing that as a kid, when I still believed in Santa Claus, and I still enjoy it, every year."

Celeste of St. Paul: "My husband, after getting out his 15-year-old Santa Claus outfit, announced that a simple pleasure is knowing that you still need a pillow to stuff yourself for Santa Claus—that he doesn't have enough natural padding, yet."

Al of Stillwater: "On Christmas Eve a few years ago, a friend of mine in St. Paul asked me to play Santa Claus for his four small children. I said, 'All right,' and I got a Santa Claus suit, and I had my son drive me over.

"On the way, we stopped at a SuperAmerica station in Stillwater to get some gas and for my son to buy a Coke, and while I was sitting in the truck—I didn't want to get out with a Santa Claus suit on—a car drove through the service area, and on the passenger side was a little girl. Her mom was driving, and as they drove by the truck, her head turned like a shot, and you could see the shock in her eyes at seeing Santa Claus sitting in a truck.

"They went over and parked, and then they came back out, and I could see the little girl just hopping up and down in her seat, pointing toward the truck and talking with her mother very animatedly. Her mother got a smile on her face, and they turned, and she deliberately drove past our truck, which was parked over a ways, and she stopped, and the little girl was hopping up and down in the seat, smiling up a storm and yelling: 'Hi, Santa Claus! Hi, Santa Claus!'

"I waved and yelled 'Merry Christmas!'—and they drove off.

"And that made my whole evening: just that little girl's shock and surprise and happiness at seeing Santa Claus in a truck and being able to say hello to Santa Claus on Christmas Eve.

It made my whole Christmas."

Sandy of St. Paul: "Today, for the first time in my whole life, when I went to the mailbox, there wasn't one ad; there wasn't one letter addressed to 'Occupant'; there wasn't one bill. It was all Christmas cards. Just lovely Christmas cards. Isn't that great?"

Marge of Eagan: "One of my simple pleasures this time of year is to pick the Christmas cards out of the mailbox and find that I have already sent cards to all of the people we just got cards from."

Al Foley of Fridley: "After going the last seven Christmases with a fake Christmas tree: having a real tree, and just coming into the house and smelling real pine."

Becky of White Bear Lake: "When you come home from school during the holiday season, and your parents have lit a beautiful fire, and all of the Christmas candles are lit, and some Christmas music is going, it's the wonderfulest feeling in the whole world."

Jodi of Richfield: "My simple pleasure is getting all my Christmas presents wrapped perfectly, with all the little bows and ribbons in their place, and put under the tree. Then I turn off all the lights, turn on the Christmas-tree lights (all 400 blinking, twinkling lights) and just sit and watch all the different colors and patterns bounce off the walls and ceiling."

Dave of Minneapolis: "I was thinking about things that have been really wonderful at Christmas, and I realized there are a whole lot of 'em; it's kinda nice to realize that your life isn't as rotten as you've been thinking it was.

"Last year, I delivered holiday baskets for the Aliveness Project, and before I made my first drop-off, I parked my car, and everything was just wonderful; it was like a music box; everything seemed just wonderfully perfect.

"When I parked my car, there were all these people streaming into the Project, and there was snow on the ground, and it was a real bright day, and it made me think of all those hokey Norman Rockwell Christmas cards that people send out, which look just ridiculously idealized—but here was something an awful lot like that that was real. It was just great seeing all these people coming to do something good."

Deb Kneen of White Bear Lake, remembering her youth: "Around Christmastime, one of our simple pleasures was being able to open the box of wrapping paper and ribbons that we used year after year after year and then carefully folded and put back in the box, to be used again the next year.

"The treat was to get the shiny navy-blue paper with the velvet ribbon. Just imagine how tattered that piece of paper must have been after being used to wrap various-size presents for five or 10 years.

"I was a preacher's kid, and we didn't have much money, but boy, I sure remember that box of wrapping paper."

Joan of St. Paul: "When I was a small girl, growing up in Tennessee, our stockings were big white socks that hung on the headboards of our beds. Oranges were really expensive this time of year; we hardly ever had 'em at our house—except, in our stockings on Christmas morning, we would always find hard candy, a nickel and an orange. And every once in a while at this time of year, when I hold an orange in my hand, I can remember what a really glorious treat it was way back then."

The Spirit in the Sky of Energy Park: " 'Tis the season for one of my simple pleasures. It's when I've been sucking on a candy cane, and I make my lips into a little O, then suck in a bunch of air or drink some water. It works with some cough drops, too, but it's much better with candy canes."

Anonymous woman: "My simple pleasure is eating more of the Christmas goodies than I should—and letting my husband believe that the kids did it."

Litch of White Bear Lake: "My simplest pleasure during the Christmas season has always been to watch 'Rudolph the Red-nosed Reindeer'—and especially hearing Clarice, a little doe, sing: 'There's always tomorrow for dreams to come true. . . .'"

Matt of Minneapolis: "My personal simple pleasure of the Christmas season is to watch 'Rudolph the Red-nosed Reindeer'—and when Santa turns to Rudolph and says, 'Won't you guide my sleigh tonight?' we always yell, at the top of our lungs: 'Buzz off, Santa!'

"Let's face it: Those reindeer were pretty cruel to Rudolph for all of his life. Santa did not step in and do a thing! Neither did the head reindeer with the whistle in his mouth; he acted like he was Mr. Joe Grade-school Hockey Coach and could do this to a poor little reindeer.

"So if we were Rudolph, we would have just said: 'Look, you guys have been complete jerks to me my entire life. Why don't you just take your sleigh and shove it!'

"Maybe that's kinda Scroogelike, but we don't think so—and we always have a really good time."

Grandpa Tom of White Bear Lake, just after Christmas: "I want everybody to know: I love my two daughters; I love my three grandchildren; and one of the highlights of my life is to have them visiting on Christmas Eve and Christmas Day.

"My simple pleasure, at this time of the year, is seeing those taillights go down the street, sitting down in my chair, and listening to the quiet. How sweet it is."

Anonymous woman of St. Paul: "One of my joys is when I'm in the car on the way to wherever I'm going on Christmas, and everything is in the car: all the food I'm supposed to make, all the presents I'm supposed to have. If I've forgotten something, I've forgotten it, and that's it. And they're playing Christmas carols, and I can just listen and enjoy and get in the mood—and not worry anymore."

R.J. of Hammond, Wis.: "I'm sitting here thinking of all that I've got yet to do today for Christmas: the grocery shopping, a couple of last cards and letters, another present to pick up, all of the presents to wrap. It'd be easy to get stressed out.

"But I'm staring at the beautiful Christmas tree, loaded with all of the ornaments that remind me of old friends and other holidays, and a wave of simple pleasure hit me: I *love* Christmas.

"I love the fresh-cut tree and all of the decorations.

"I love the cards and letters and pictures from friends and family, and the way Christmas keeps us in touch.

"I love the planning and the shopping and the secrets.

"I love this beautiful snow, and Christmas carols, and all the great Christmas music written down through the ages.

"I love the church service on Christmas Eve, and the old, familiar words of the Nativity story.

"And the excitement of the little kids right now.

"And driving down a dark road at night, and coming on a tree or a house all lit up—simple or elaborate, doesn't matter.

"And that's what this is all about: giving, and loving one another, and hope, and joy, and a light shining in the darkness to ease our burdens and dispel the gloom forever.

"It's about a drab, weary, mean world, just like ours today, that was transformed by magic, once upon a time, and every year thereafter. So don't worry about *making* it happen, folks; *let* it happen.

"Just concentrate on putting a smile on your face and the faces of your loved ones.

"Merry Christmas, everybody."

SIMPLE PLEASURES OF
The Home

Marty of St. Paul: "I just took down the Merry Christmas knitted wall-hanging rug thing from above the fireplace, and I'm replacing it with my stuffed fish—back in its rightful resting place, for all to see. It's gonna be a great year."

Webby of Minneapolis: "I just walked into my house, and the whole damn thing is clean. Sparklin' clean. My simple pleasure is when my big toad of a roommate finally gets around to cleanin' up the place—out of the blue.

"And it's snowing, too; it's a beautiful, beautiful thing. It's a beautiful country we live in. God bless America!

"See how happy it makes me?"

Kimberly of River Falls, Wis.: "My simple pleasure is putting in a clean vacuum bag in my new vacuum cleaner and suckin' up all this nasty dirt and grit and dog hair that seems to accumulate faster in the winter—because it's so disgusting!"

Kathy of St. Paul: "I like to vacuum. When you get the tracks from the vacuum cleaner nice and even and straight in the plush carpet, it makes the room look so nice and clean that you don't even notice the dust."

Nancy of Lakeville: "Walking barefoot on a nice, freshly washed and waxed floor. Very nice."

Scott of St. Paul: "My wife Theresa's strange simple pleasure is to walk into the kitchen while the dishwasher is going, to stop the dishwasher in the middle of the cycle, to open it up and take deep, deep breaths, smelling the deliciousness of the soap. She enjoys that as a simple pleasure for two reasons: (1) It smells hot and clean; and (2) it reminds her that somebody other than her is doing the dishes."

Big Steve of St. Paul: "A fresh, new bottle of dish soap. You know, after a week of shaking and squeezing and banging that empty bottle on the sink, trying to get those last few drops out of the bottle, the next day—when you've got that full bottle of soap, and all you do is pop the top and give her one squeeze: Ahhhhhh, that's a pleasure."

Anonymous woman: "Reading about Big Steve's simple pleasure made me think that my simple pleasure would be actually having a man in my life who did housework. Gotta love it."

Wende of West St. Paul: "A *real* simple pleasure is sitting there washing the walls with your ex-boyfriend's undershorts—and seein' the walls come clean, which is more than *he* ever did."

Louie of Maplewood—a man who presumably bathes alone: "Say, for a simple pleasure: gettin' up in the morning and havin' a chew in the shower—because you can spit on the floor, the wall or even yourself, and it doesn't matter."

Heidi of Roseville: "When I get up and get into the shower and I pick up the soap—and there are no hairs on it."

Curt of Apple Valley: "The most underrated simple pleasure in this country is a hot shower. People just don't realize how fortunate they are to routinely bathe in hot water."

BULLETIN BOARD ADDS: *Even if the walls are dotted with spittle and the soap is beyond hope.*

Jan of Maplewood: "I have what I call a Miracle Pleasure. It would be a pleasure—and a miracle if it ever happened—to walk into my bathroom and see that somebody else has cleaned it. I mean, really cleaned it: scrubbed the toilet, scrubbed the tub shiny, and cleaned up all the hair on the floor."

Pat of Roseville: "I like to put the toilet-paper roll on, because I like making a fresh roll unroll—and I get to put it on the right way."

Susan of Eagan: "A simple pleasure, after changing a dirty diaper—and anyone with kids would know this: opening the diaper pail and being able to drop the diaper in and hear it hit the bottom, rather than have the diaper pail be full and try to squish another one in or have to put in another bag."

Carrie of Baldwin, Wis.: "I love to stand there and just watch the water going around and around in my washer as it agitates, and all this crud comes out of my clothes and makes the water really dirty. I just love to watch that, because I know all that crud is coming out of my clothes and down the drain."

Suzanne of Eagan: "Washing a load of wash, going to throw it in the dryer, and finding the dryer empty."

Terry of Stillwater: "I love to hang clothes outside on the clothesline. The job itself is sort of therapeutic; simple motions in the fresh air are calming. During the day, I like to look outside and watch the clothes blowing in the breeze. It's very satisfying, for some reason. And sleeping on freshly aired sheets is heavenly."

Deep in the Heart of Como: "My simple pleasure is climbing up to clean out the gutters and finding nothing there to clean out."

Kris of Stillwater: "Today, when I cleaned out my refrigerator, I didn't find anything moldy or foul-smelling. That is definitely a simple pleasure."

J.D. of White Bear Lake: "My favorite thing is when I open up the freezer door. I look in there, and we have an icemaker, and the icemaker pops out the ice in little rows, and I love taking the rows and smashin' 'em over the top of the glass, so they break just perfectly into little pieces into the glass. That's the coolest thing in the world."

Jean of St. Paul: "A pleasant moment is when all of the crumbs fall out of a toaster when you shake it. So nice."

Pat of St. Paul: "I hate painting—inside or outside or anything—but the one thing that I do like about it is when you get that roller all full of paint, and you put it on the wall, and you start running it up and down, and it makes that sticky, sucky sound. That almost makes painting worthwhile—but probably not quite."

Todd of St. Paul: "One of life's little pleasures, for me, is to paint the rooms in my house in the buff. The paint drips on you, and you can just wash it all off. It's a lot of fun, and if you have a date over who's helping you paint, it can be very interesting."

Andrea of Woodbury: "I was over at my girlfriend Stacey's house—by the way, she's an avid Bullboard . . . Billboard! . . . or Bullboard [Andrea laughs] reader as well. [BULLETIN BOARD NOTES: *That's Bulletin Board. Thank you.*] We were peeling wallpaper off in one of her closets, and it was coming off in chunks about the size of a dime. We were getting extremely frustrated, so we moved to the bathroom, and in there, we were peeling wallpaper off in nice, big sheets.

"Stacey looked at me and said: 'You know what this is?' And we said: 'It's a simple pleasure!'"

Sandy W. of Little Canada: "After years of remodeling an older house, we built a new house a couple of years ago—and although it's not fancy, it is new. So when a remodeler calls to try to sell me windows or siding, my simple pleasure is to say: 'I don't need any of that. I've got a new house. Thank you.'"

Blue Petal of Minneapolis: "When I get up in the morning or come home at night and take a look around the outside of the house and discover that there's no new vandalism, no new graffiti, no new broken windows, no break-ins of the garage—that's my simple pleasure. I wish it happened more often."

Kerry of Mahtomedi: "My simple pleasure is coming home from a hard day's work and having my husband cooking dinner —and that smell when you walk in the door, of garlic or butter or onions or something cookin'. Smells so darn good, and it just makes you feel so comfortable and happy to be home. You know what I mean?"

Missy of Mahtomedi: "I work nights. I bartend. So I got home at 2 o'clock this morning, and I tucked in my daughters —they were sleeping, and they're so sweet when they're asleep—and I went into my bedroom to lay down, and it was really dark, and my dog was really happy to see me, and he jumped up on the bed, and he was rollin' all around because he was so excited . . . and you could see the static electricity, the sparks comin' off. It was really cool.

"But now, of course, all that's changed. My daughters are screaming at each other, and my dog's in the kennel because he jumped up on the table. But it was quite a pleasure last night."

D.H. of Exeland, Wis.: "Among my simple pleasures are a good cup of coffee, a good cigar, and Schubert, or Mozart, or Bach on the CD—as I live in a three-room shack with a dog that I do not sleep with."

Peabody the Paper Pelican of White Bear Lake: "I really like it when you make a big, long list of Things to Do—and when you cross off the very last Thing on it, it's the best thing in the world . . . almost.

"There's one feeling that's better: It's when someone you love says 'I love you' without you saying it first—just right out of the blue."

SIMPLE PLEASURES OF
Love

Pupster of St. Paul: "When I'm really lucky at work and my day is going just completely awesome, I run into this guy up on the sixth floor—and he has the most magnificent smile that I've ever seen in my entire life, and the clearest, bluest eyes. My heart just melts. I'm kinda hoping he doesn't have a girlfriend, because I really want to ask him out—but if he does, my only hope is that she realizes what a treasure she has."

T.J. of St. Paul: "There's a guy that I like at school, and every time I'm walking down the hall and see him unexpectedly, I get these tingles. They're so wonderful."

M.T. of St. Paul: "I just got my first kiss, and it's really great. I'm already 15, and a lot of my friends have been kissing since, like, sixth grade—but I decided to wait, and I'm really glad I did, because I just like this guy so much.

"Nothing beats getting your first kiss."

The Bookwoman of St. Paul: "I have a response to the young lady whose simple pleasure was receiving her first kiss, at 15:

"I hate to admit it, but I am approaching middle age and have not had a wonderful man in my life for quite a while. I recently met a wonderful man—and those simple pleasures don't go away. Holding hands at a movie is wonderful, and the kisses are just as sweet as they were at 15.

"So my advice to that young lady is: Don't ever lose that magic. It will always be a simple pleasure."

Denise of Little Canada: "One of the best things about kissing is the butterflies you feel."

Denise's Friend Laurie of Little Canada, moments later: "It's the next day, after the first kiss in a new relationship, and you still feel the butterflies."

Brian of parts undisclosed: "I'm surprised no one has mentioned sex as one of the simple pleasures."

BULLETIN BOARD REPLIES: *Doesn't surprise us a bit. We've never known anyone who thought it was simple.*

Becky of the East Side: "Finding out that the guy I've been dating for two weeks is nothing more than a con artist, a liar and a cheat. The simple pleasure in that is discovering it not four months down the line, six months down the line—when I'm an emotional wreck over the jerk."

Jenny B. of Woodbury: "Walking into a place where my ex-boyfriend is, with a gorgeous guy on my arm."

Nancy of St. Paul: "A really great back rub from someone who loves you a lot and really puts a lot of effort into it—the kind my husband used to give me before we got married."

Karen of Shoreview: "Every morning, my husband has a cup of coffee waiting for me when I get out of bed. He travels a lot for work, but on the days he is home, I get that cup of coffee—no matter what a crab I've been to live with."

Jaz of Isanti: "One of my favorite simple pleasures is me and my boyfriend poppin' in a movie in the VCR on a Friday or Saturday night and pickin' up some crab legs, meltin' lots of butter, climbin' into bed and watchin' our movie and eatin' our crab legs."

Bashful of Burnsville: "A simple pleasure from the old days, when we were dating and courting before marriage—in contrast to the one you had where the couple was eating buttered crab legs in bed. Our simple pleasure was to pop a giant bowl of popcorn and share it as we watched the late-night movie. And then, when we were too tired to stay awake any longer, we'd kiss goodnight and I'd send my boyfriend home.

"Then, when we were married and had a son and a daughter, our simple pleasure changed into two bowls of buttered popcorn—each parent in a rocker/recliner with a kid on their lap—and Pepsi, and then we'd sit and watch and enjoy the Disney movies on Sunday. Shows a big difference in lifestyles, I guess."

The Happy Homemaker of the eastern suburbs: "I was huggin' my honey on Mother's Day and realized that the very best thing of all about being married 12½ years is that everything fits somewhere. There's a spot just underneath his chin, in that little hollow place, where my head fits, and then my shoulder fits right next to his armpit. And when we're sleepin', there's a special spot where my foot fits next to his. Everything has a place, and it feels so . . . cozy. I hope everybody gets to experience something like that in their life."

Linda W. of Eagan: "I have an extra-special pleasure. My husband, Scott, went fishing, and I received one dozen long-stemmed red roses while he's been gone. I love him so much, and I miss him like crazy, and I hope he catches a big walleye and gets back real soon."

Chillon of St. Paul: "I'm calling about a more-than-simple pleasure—and that is: looking out your window on a cold spring day and seeing a florist's truck drive up, and then realizing that the delivery man is coming to your door. And if that isn't wonderful enough, it's opening the letter that accompanies this incredible bouquet and finding out it's from your husband, who understands more than anybody what it's like to be a stay-at-home mom with three little kids and a new puppy."

Jennifer of St. Paul: "My boyfriend left for Denver this morning, and I came home and the house is so quiet. There's no TV, no radio, no guitars, no drums.

"We've been together four years, and I don't think we've ever been apart for more than a couple of days. And this is just wonderful! It's just quiet and peaceful, and I'm sitting here reading the Bulletin Board, and my dog is here, and my cats are here—and they hide when he's home, because they don't like him. (He's just incredibly loud, and they have very sensitive ears.)

"So we're all curled up on the couch, and it's just great. It's a very simple pleasure—to have your boyfriend gone, but you know that you love him and he loves you and he'll be back."

Aaron of St. Paul: "I came back from a trip to Chicago—and had my girlfriend waitin' for me at the airport. It was special 'cause I haven't had a girlfriend for a long time. Kinda simple, but it was romantic—just like you see in Hollywood. I was the last person off the airplane, and there she was—smilin', waitin' for me."

SIMPLE PLEASURES OF
Family

Sharon of Eagan: "I wanted to tell you my greatest simple pleasure in the world: It's when my baby daughter Brooke falls asleep on my lap, and I'm sittin' there lookin' at her, and suddenly, in her sleep, she gets this big smile on her face. Oh, it's beautiful. It means everything in her world, at least, is happy and peaceful."

BULLETIN BOARD NOTES: *And before Sharon hung up, we could hear a gurgling, laughing baby. Happy and peaceful.*

Mary of White Bear Lake: "Last week, my 6-month-old daughter decided to wake up at 2:30 in the morning, to eat and then to play. We were on the floor playing for about an hour, and I was trying hard to keep my eyes open while Theresa was laughing and playing with her toys. I was lying down, with my eyes half-open, and she's watching me—and the next thing I know, she crawls over, poking at my closed eyelids.

"She snuggled up alongside me and made a few heavy sighs—and I looked down a few minutes later, and she was sound asleep, right alongside me. It was so sweet, and I'll always treasure that special moment."

Celeste of St. Paul: "When my 10-month-old wakes up at 4 or 5 in the morning—this is after 10 or 11 hours of sleep, so it's not that bad—and I'm able to feed him and rock him and make him comfortable enough to go back to sleep, I always think of all the poor mothers in Somalia who don't have food for their babies, and how horrible it must be for them to hear their babies cry and cry and not be able to do anything about it.

"I always feel lucky to be here, in Minnesota, in the United States—even if it is 5 in the morning."

D.R.K. of Mac-Groveland: "When I do something and my little girl gets this belly laugh and starts laughing so hard, it's the best thing in the world."

BULLETIN BOARD REPLIES: *Especially when you compare it with the semi-screaming we heard in the background, presumably from the same little girl.*

Allison of Cannon Falls: "I have a 2-year-old, a 3-year-old and a 4-year-old—and my favorite words are 'nap time.'"

Mommy of White Bear Lake: "Mine is when I put my little babies to bed at night, and long after they go to sleep, I go in to check on 'em, and I cover 'em and snuggle up and say 'I love you'—and they mumble 'I love you, too, Mommy.' That's just the neatest thing in the whole world."

Sally the Cleaning Lady of Shoreview: "My baby will soon be 17, and I still love to kiss her good night and tell her I love her long after she's gone to sleep. She usually sleeps through it, now, but every now and then, she mumbles: 'I love you, too.' It will always delight me."

Leah of Minneapolis: "I experienced two simple pleasures last week. When I carried my 12-week-old son from the car to his crib without waking him up, I remembered what a simple pleasure it was to be carried from the car after a long day of shopping or visiting relatives and be snuggled into my bed without having to wake up. And then, like most simple pleasures I've recalled since becoming a new mom, I realized it's even better to carry than to be carried."

Alyssa of the East Side: "My baby's cutting her first teeth, and I'm so proud of her. I know it's stupid, but obviously I'm a first-time mother, and it just makes me so proud. I've called everyone I know, and I've driven over to grandma and grandpa's houses, and friends' houses, to make 'em feel those teeth.

"My husband thinks I'm a geek—but it makes me happy."

Jennifer of St. Paul: "I love it when I see parents taking time to let their kids enjoy things—little, simple things. I was out on break at work, and there were a bunch of geese across the road, with their babies. And I saw this man pull over to the side of the road with a carload of kids, just to stop and let the kids see the geese. I thought that was really neat."

Terri of White Bear Lake: "The neighbors were giving away a free king-size waterbed. So we took it; I thought it'd be a great idea to set it up in the basement for one of those hot summer nights we used to have. What we all do is: The whole family grabs their pillows and piles on the bed when there's something great on TV that we all want to watch. We're joined by one or two of the dogs and one or two of the cats—and then Glory, our pot-bellied pig, joins us. That's really a true pleasure."

Papa Bear of Hastings: "At 4:30 New Year's morning, our 5-month-old woke us up, miserable with a cold. My wife fixed up some saline drops and fed the baby while I made coffee. Then the three of us went downstairs, made a nest on the couch, and popped in a video we were too tired to watch on New Year's Eve.

"Two hours later, I'm sitting here thinking what a wonderful simple pleasure this is. Our baby is sleeping peacefully in my arms, little hand clutching a fistful of chest hair. My wife, at the other end of the couch, wrapped in a blanket, a cup of coffee in her hand, our dog lying at her feet. The house is quiet. Our two big boys are still asleep upstairs. We are all cozy and content and warm and together.

"What a great way to start out a whole new year."

C.J. of St. Paul: "My kids just recently discovered those old Little Rascals movies. So we go to the movie store and rent a couple, and we'll snuggle on the couch and just laugh and laugh together. You know, I kinda forgot how funny they really are. Good, clean, cheap entertainment."

J. of St. Paul: "A simple pleasure that I discovered last night: books from my childhood that I'm now reading to my children. It's neat, because I have 'em in my mind the way I remember them, and now I'm reading 'em again and I see 'em in a different light—and I really enjoy watching my kids enjoy 'em, too."

The Newcomer of St. Paul: "My simple pleasure is waking up in the morning, opening the blinds over the head of our bed, and watching my 4-year-old and 1-year-old daughters lie on their tummies on our pillows while they look out the window into our neighbor's beautiful garden.

"Recently, we watched a little rabbit hop around the garden for a good 15 minutes or so. I got such a kick out of watching them get such a kick out of watching the rabbit."

Mike of Mac-Grove: "To me, one of the simple pleasures in life is just enjoying the new perspective that kids can bring to your life—about things that you just take for granted.

"I had all the kids out camping last week, and my 5-year-old son and I are standing there looking up at the sky, and the sky is really full of stars, and the quarter-moon was right on the horizon, so it was really big and really orange, and my son says: 'Look, Dad. The sun's smiling at us.'

"I'll always think of the quarter-moon that way, from now on. Just something that only a kid could say."

Mary of Mahtomedi: "Watching my 4^1/$_2$-year-old tie his shoes. He just learned this week, and watching this action that we all take so much for granted being done in slow . . . and deliberate . . . and painstaking . . . and careful . . . and mind-cog-grinding steps is just a delightful process to watch.

"But it's accompanied by what I suppose you'd call a simple displeasure in life, and that is: watching him do that when you're already late for whatever it is you're trying to get to, and knowing that he'll scream bloody murder if you try to intervene, and watching that slow . . . and painstaking process . . . take place . . . as the meter ticks . . .

"But it's precious; it really is."

Lovely Rita Meter Maid of Dakota County: "I was getting ready for work, and my first-grader woke up and went in the bathroom. Pretty soon I heard her shout: 'Mom, come here!'—as if something was wrong.

"I hurried to the bathroom and opened the door. She had an excited and proud look on her face and exclaimed: 'Mom, three plus two equals five!' I said: 'Yes, that's right!'

"After thinking that she might be sick or something, I felt an immediate sense of relief and said that myself: 'Now that's a simple pleasure if I've ever had one!'

"Unexpected simple pleasures are even better than regular simple pleasures."

Amy of the East Side: "Last year, I quit my full-time job so that I could be home for a year with my little girl before she goes to school.

"Needless to say, we've had to make a lot of sacrifices to make this work. But I was just sitting out on the steps, and it's a beautiful day—winter's finally gone—and I've been teaching my little girl, for the last week, how to ride her bike without training wheels, and she just finally got it.

"She's cruisin' along up the street, laughin' and smilin' and happy, and suddenly I realized I was just sitting there like an idiot, smiling my face off, with tears pouring down my face."

L.S.R. of Stacy: "My simple pleasure is hearing my grand-daughter Molly's footsteps. She'll be 4 years old on February 23rd. Molly is hydrocephalic and has just learned to walk. The prognosis was that she would be in a wheelchair, or maybe crawl. Thanks, God, and way to go, Molly. We love ya."

Grandma Dorothy of Lake Elmo: "Under the heading of life's most wonderful joys: There's no way to even describe it; it's when you go see *your* baby and she puts *her* baby in your arms for the first time. And that, Jack, is what it's all about."

Harry of Round Lake, Wis.: "A simple pleasure: if I'm walking with my grandson and he—for no reason, really—takes my hand."

Barefoot and Pregnant of Maplewood, with a hot sax in the distant background: "I like to sneak up on my husband and son when they're downstairs in our rec room and watch them dance to crazy music—like they're doing right now! Hear? . . . Well, even if you can't, they're having a good time."

Leslie of Forest Lake: "My simple pleasure is when I hear my son Kyle say: 'Hey, Dad, let's make some music.' He's 10 years old, and he goes over to the piano and starts to play, and my husband grabs his bass. I've driven my son to piano lessons for five years in order to hear him say that."

Katie of White Bear Lake: "My simple pleasure is when every time I talk about how I like country music, my mother gets this disgusted look on her face—like she's thinking, 'Where did I go wrong?' I just laugh and laugh about it."

Babycakes of Oakdale: "My simple pleasure is when you've been working all night, and you come home to find that your mom has taped '90210' and 'Melrose' for you."

BULLETIN BOARD REPLIES: *That is true love.*

Red of Oakdale: "My simple pleasure is watching MTV's 'Beavis and Butt-head' with my son and laughing out loud, knowing full well that nobody else knows that I'm watching it—unless my son tells on me, of course."

Neruse of Inver Grove Heights: "One of my simple pleasures is fighting with my brother and not getting in trouble for it."

K.T. of Wisconsin: "I'm calling with one of my simple pleasures—which, most of the time, turns out to be not very simple, but it's definitely the greatest. And that is: closing the door behind my children as they leave for school."

Kathy of St. Paul: "Every few weeks, when my son gets out of kindergarten in the morning, the two of us go to a local bakery. We sit at a little table, eating our doughnuts, while he describes his morning activities in school.

"These private outings cost $1.50, but they're worth a million dollars to me. I think that's a simple pleasure."

Ken of Newport: "It's nighttime; I've just come home from working second shift.

"The house is quiet; my kids are asleep; I go through and tuck 'em back in, put their covers around 'em; sit down; read my newspaper, finishing up with Bulletin Board; and I also go through all the stuff my kids bring home from school every day.

"My 10-year-old daughter, Erin, had written this piece for Martin Luther King Day. It's titled 'He Had a Dream, and So Do I.' It states: 'I have a dream that people will not hate, but only love. I have a dream that all the people will have food to eat and water to drink. My dream is that I could take all the hatred in the world and throw it in the trash. My dream is that some people will not hate people because they are black or white. I think people who kill with guns should stop and not have them, because killing is wrong, not right. I have a dream that people will not be so prejudiced.'

"It's a simple pleasure that fills me with a lot of pride."

Charly of St. Paul: "The other day, I was feeling kind of blue because it was my last day at a job I truly loved. And my 9-year-old boy took his only $2, walked over to Holiday and surprised me with a red rose to cheer me up."

Curly Top of Le Sueur: "One of my simple pleasures occurred when I took my 18-year-old daughter Christmas shopping. In her usual teenage eagerness, she jumped out of the car ahead of me while I was locking it up, and was rushing to get into the shopping center as soon as possible. But I saw her stop at the Salvation Army's bell-ringer, dig in her purse and put some money in the pot.

"It really warmed my heart to see her do that without any prompting."

Freshman of Eagan: "My mama has the flu, and along with feeling horrible, she has all the other symptoms—like the chills. So my simple pleasure is washing and drying her sheets and putting 'em on her bed really warm, so when she gets in her bed from off the couch, she's really warm, and she doesn't have the chills anymore."

A.C. of White Bear Lake: "I have Savings Bonds payroll-deducted every paycheck. I have $25 taken out of every paycheck, so every month, I get a $100 savings bond. My fiancée and I are intending to use these for our future children's college funds.

"My simple pleasure is that every month, when I get another

$100 savings bond, I count up all of the ones I have and think: 'That's how much money I have for our children's college funds.' And what's more, our children aren't even born yet, so by the time they're ready for college, that's gonna be quite a college fund. That really makes me happy, every time I count 'em up."

Bob of Rochester: "I got a call Sunday from my daughter, Coleen, in Mexico saying she was coming home for a surprise visit. My wife, Jane, was working, so I dropped in on her at work. I asked her, 'If you could have anything in the world, what would it be?' Without a second's hesitation, she said, 'To see Coleen.'

"That's my simple pleasure—that she would choose that over money or anything else.

"The second simple pleasure was watching the tears come to her eyes when I told her: 'Well, you can . . . tomorrow night.'"

Louise of St. Paul: "My simple pleasure is playing Scrabble with my mother in her sunny dining room. We don't care who wins; my goal is to cover all of the red triple-word spaces and to have the words spread out all over the board. I even take pictures of especially good game boards.

"During the game, my mom often reminisces about her childhood, growing up in the West Seventh Street area: Sunday drives and family picnics; what her family ate for dinner (meat and potatoes every day); how my grandmother would put the potatoes on when she heard the closing whistle in the railroad yard where my grandpa worked. She tells how ice-cream cones were a once-a-month treat, and the fun of watching the lamplighters light the street lamps.

"It's a very special sharing time—a time I will always treasure."

Becky of Bethel College, speaking of her grandpa: "The oldest of his seven grandchildren is 21, and the youngest is a year old. Every week of every year since we were born, he writes each one of us a letter. I love seeing that green envelope in my mail every week."

Sarah the Scholar of Rutgers University: "A good belly laugh is one of my greatest simple pleasures—and one that I don't experience very often these days, as I'm in the throes of graduate school in New Jersey. But in this difficult time, one of my great treasures is an audio tape on which is recorded my great-aunt, Helen Flynn, who died 10 years ago, telling stories about her childhood, and laughing the most wonderful laugh, and my parents and brother and me laughing in the background, and even our beloved dogs, now dead also, growling at each other under the table—and it just makes me smile to hear it, and reminds me of what's really important."

Joe of Brooklyn Park: "I've got a simple pleasure. It's when my 3½-year-old son comes up to me and says: 'You're my best pal in the whole wide world.'"

Sharon of St. Paul: "How can you put into words this feeling? My 11-year-old son, who is autistic, comes up behind me, puts his arms around my waist, and gives me a hug. Oooooh, what a rush."

Jo E. of Stillwater: "I'm reading here about some advances they're making with cystic fibrosis. My simple pleasure is just knowing that these things are going on, because my daughter has cystic fibrosis, and my grandson has cystic fibrosis. Who says God doesn't answer prayers?"

Cheesecake of Stillwater: "Holding babies is a blessed, God-given pleasure. My sister has a very severely brain-damaged baby, and we love her a lot. And the best we can do for her is to hold her. She can't cry; she can't talk to us—but she knows when she's being held, and it's the best thing in the world.

"We're not gonna have this baby for very long; she'll leave us soon—but we're gonna hold her as long as we can.

"So, moms, enjoy your babies; hold 'em as much as you can."

BULLETIN BOARD NOTES: *You dads, too.*

SIMPLE PLEASURES OF
The Seasons

Jody of St. Paul: "My simple pleasure this past week has been walking home from work and listening to the melting snow running down the gutters into the sewers. It's music to the ears of someone who's been walking to work all this long, frozen winter."

Rob of Eagan: "I built an eight-foot snowman with my brother-in-law over last weekend, and it is slowly tilting to one side, melting, falling away. My simple pleasure is coming home from work every day and seeing how much closer to the ground it is getting."

G.F. of parts hereabouts: "As amazing as it was last winter to come home at night and listen to the lake freeze up out front, it's even nicer, in a way, that each day when I go out, and each evening when I come home, the open spot in the lake right out in front of the place here is getting bigger and bigger and bigger.

"An acoustic pleasure is hearing the geese honking away down there at night and knowing they're back for the spring."

Elaine of the East Side: "It gives me a nice, secure feeling, knowing that these beautiful geese come back to the same pond year after year, and you see the mothers ushering their babies across the street."

Brandi of Rochester: "The days are getting longer—so that when I wake up in the morning, it's actually bright. In fact, today I thought I had overslept, because when I woke up, the sun was shining so bright in my room."

Marie of St. Paul: "Being able to open the window for the fresh air. The cats come leaping up onto the windowsill to perch and watch the birds; we all get to sit and hear the birds tweet. What a joy."

Kathy of Zimmerman: "Today I was able to go outside and eat the sweet icicles off of the maple trees. On a frosty morning, as the sap rises, these wonderful icicles form that are sweet—and it reminds me of my childhood."

Mommy B. of "somewhere north of White Bear": "I was vacuuming, and everything was humming along—and all of a sudden, I sucked up a pile of sand. Yes, it's spring! The snow is off the sandbox, and my preschoolers have been outside."

Mommy of Hastings: "Sitting in the sunshine in the backyard with my four little boys, watching them relish the first Popsicles of the season."

S.O.B. (Sweet Old Bill) of Maplewood: "Go out and find a creek, and pick your own watercress. That's what spring is all about."

Kirsten of Falcon Heights: "My honest-to-God simple pleasure is smelling dirt in the springtime. I never realize how much I don't like winter 'til springtime comes around."

Margie of Roseville: "A freshly tilled garden, just ready to be planted."

Susan of Falcon Heights: "Going to the farmers' market and buying all that beautiful produce, and then I bring it home and wash it and lay it all out on the counter and look at all the beautiful colors."

Mary of Little Canada: "Sitting on the deck of our cabin on a lovely summer evening, with our dog lying beside me, watching the sun set across the lake while I listen to the waves lapping on the shore and a Brahms symphony on public radio."

Mudskipper of Stillwater: "Warm summer nights when you have wonderful thunderstorms with lightning—just sitting at my window with it completely black out, sitting and listening to the rain. It's so incredibly relaxing."

A.L. of St. Paul: "Sitting out on a nice, breezy, summer evening, and hearing the wind softly rustling through the trees, and listening to those little crickets chirpin' away."

Suburban Girl of, well . . . the suburbs, we suppose: "Sleeping on a hot summer night with the windows wide open, listening to the crickets sing and the semis downshifting on the highway two blocks away. Beats the heck out of air conditioning."

Snippy of Hudson: "When my sister, Gypsy Woman, is vacuuming her car and the mosquitoes are about to suck her blood, she likes to suck them up with the vacuum cleaner."

Terri of Mosquitoville: "A simple pleasure: It's when I slap mosquitoes and I can hear 'em hit the floor."

Becky of Woodbury: "On a really hot day, when you get a bad sunburn, you put a jar of Noxzema in the refrigerator and put it on. I love the smell, and it feels so good."

Jim of South St. Paul: "When you get a good sunburn, and a week later your skin starts to peel, you can sit there for hours at a time, peeling off skin. Every once in a while, you just get that giant piece of skin that comes off so nice."

Mary of White Bear Lake: "When my sister's sunburn starts to peel, she lets me pull off the sheets of dead skin."

Kewpie Doll of Isanti: "Years ago, I discovered that one of my greatest pleasures was when it was really, really hot and you just couldn't get any relief from fans or anything. About three hours before bedtime, I would take my pillow and put it in my freezer and leave it in there, and then when it came time to go to bed, I'd pull it out of there. It was just perfect, just wonderful."

Mike of St. Paul (echoed by *C&J* of St. Paul): "When defrosting the freezer in the summer, tapping the overhead ice and having it come off in one piece. Even if it crashes to the bottom and fractures into a thousand ice crystals, you can still make and throw snowballs in the summer."

Nipper of White Bear Lake, an employee of a fast-food chain: "After working an 11-hour shift: lying out on the baseball field at the high school, watching the shooting stars with my friends. It kinda makes me think that somebody out there likes me, after all."

Big Man, Big Man of White Bear Lake, another fast-food worker: "Sometimes, I'm over the grill, cooking this big burger-type ultimate thing, and somebody opens both doors on one side, and this rush of cool air comes in. To stand there for, like, five seconds going 'Aaaaahhh' in the cool air—that's my simple pleasure."

Joyce of St. Paul: "I had a simple pleasure this morning. As I walked outside to go to the garage, around 6:45, I heard a noise—and what it was was leaves falling off the trees. So I stood there for about two minutes and listened to leaves fall off my trees. It was still dark, and there were still stars—and it was very nice."

John of St. Paul: "The high winds of the last few days have produced that peculiarly autumnal aural phenomenon—the comforting, clattering rattle of dried leaves bouncing over the pavement or skittering into the air. The next rain (or snow) will probably silence them, and that sound will be gone until next year. I miss the smell of burning leaves, but this distinctive mark of fall remains."

Monkey Girl of St. Paul: "When I walk home from school, I really like walking through the dead, crunchy leaves on the ground and making that crackling noise. It's so much fun."

Cookie of Eagan: "We were up at the cabin last weekend, and I rediscovered one of the greatest pleasures in life: jumping into an absolutely humongous pile of leaves. There's nothing better on a sunny autumn afternoon. The thing that made it even better this time was that I had my 2-year-old and my 6-year-old with me, and it's just a blast being a kid again with your own two kids."

Shirl of St. Paul: "My simple pleasure is watching my leaves blow down the block. My not-so-pleasant pleasure is watching them when they blow back up the block."

Diane of St. Paul Park: "I do day care, so my days are generally quite noisy. I always make it a point of waking up about an hour earlier than I really need to, just so I can have some quiet time before my day begins.

"I make a nice hot cup of cappuccino, and I go out on my porch, all by myself in the cool breeze. And that hot cup feels really good in my not-so-warm hands. It's so quiet and relaxing, just listening to the wind blowing through the trees, watching the changing leaves fall to the ground, smelling fall smells.

"This morning was really perfect, because one of the neighbors must have had a fire going in his fireplace, and you could smell the wood burning."

"When I'm in the middle of my day, and my kids are being not so quiet, I think back to the quiet time I had that morning—and somehow, that gets me through my day."

Donna of Rice Lake: "Here's one for you: sitting high up in my tree stand, with a lovely soft snow quietly falling around me, dunking chocolate-chunk—not just chip; chocolate-chunk—cookies in hot, steamy coffee from my Thermos, knowing it's the last day of the deer season, knowing I'm the only one of six who's gotten a deer, knowing I'm the only one of six who's a female, and knowing that there are 355 days left to rub it in before the next season starts.

"Lots of little pleasures make for big simple pleasures."

Deb of Stillwater: "I was reading about this guy sitting up in a tree, and he'd gotten his deer. [BULLETIN BOARD INTERJECTS: *Actually, that was a woman in her tree who, unlike the five men she was with, had gotten her deer—and her simple pleasure was that she had 355 days to rub it in before they'd get another chance.*] My husband's a bow hunter, and he'd been hunting for months and hadn't gotten one yet.

"He was hunting one day, and he came home and said: 'Well, I didn't get a deer.' I said: 'I'd believe that one.' And he said: 'But it was better. I was sitting there, and I had four trumpeter swans fly overhead. It was the most beautiful thing I've ever seen.'

"That's a simple pleasure."

Grandma Up North: "We've had a weekend that has been, honestly, a miracle—because we live in the North Country, as you know, and to have a weekend like this is so spectacular, so incredibly undeserved.

"A friend and I were talking, and she said, 'Gee, I wish we could bottle it. Put it in a jar.'

"And I thought: Why not? So I cleaned out a jar, the cap and everything, and went out in the back yard. Twirled around three times, to get the air in there really good, and then clamped it shut. Then I came in and glued it shut. I wrote on it: 'This jar contains beautiful air from a perfect day, October 24, 1993.'

"I told my friend Pat about it, and she said she'd like a jar, too. She said it just in time, because the sun was declining. I rushed out and caught it just in time—one degree less than it was before, but it was pretty good.

"So this very dark and dreary winter, she'll be able to take that jar out and look at it, and it will say, 'Contents: 65 degrees, sunny sky, no wind, perfect.' I think that's pretty good.

"And not only that, there's only two jars in existence."

Susie of Arden Hills: "I'm in the kitchen, and I'm making dinner, and I've got my little TV on to the news, and the snow is falling, and they're showing pictures of children on their sleds and laying in the snow making angels—and I just had to stop and watch, and I got big tears in my eyes, remembering how much fun it was to take my kids out and lay in the snow with them and feel how good it feels in all that fluff."

Becca of Frogtown: "A simple pleasure: having a boyfriend who likes to play in the snow as much as I do. We like to go out and catch snowflakes on our tongues, or get in big snowball fights, or just go for long, long walks. It's funny: As long as he's with me, I'm never cold."

Reno of Shoreview: "I'm a bartender, and I work nights, and coming home tonight from work, I noticed that in the streetlights and the moonlight, all of the new snow on the streets sparkles like glitter. It is absolutely beautiful."

Stardust of Arden Hills: "My simple pleasure is something that I've loved ever since I was a kid. When the snowplow would come by, I'd always run to the window to watch it—because the sparks fly up from the blade scraping against the pavement. I think that's really cool—especially at night."

Katherine of Stacy: "The frost on the windows on very, very cold mornings looks like pretty ferns growing on your windows, and if the sun shines on the pretty frost, it's just like diamonds."

Elizabeth of White Bear Lake: "I remember going ice-skating, and coming home and having my toes absolutely frozen, and popping off my boots and sitting on the floor and sticking my feet between the sections of a hot radiator."

Katherine of St. Paul: "I'm calling to give you a simple pleasure from my childhood. I remembered it one day last week, when I got up and padded to the bathroom, and the floor was cold, and I looked around for the furnace register for our forced-air heat and realized it was all the way across the bathroom, by the towels, and it reminded me of when I was a little girl, and I'd get up in the winter and it would be so cold, and I'd run to the bathroom, where the furnace register was right underneath the sink—and if you were lucky, you got there to brush your teeth and wash your face just when the heat kicked on, and you could stand there forever brushing your teeth, having all that wonderful warm air go over your toes and make you feel good and warm. That used to be my little way of telling if it was going to be a good day or not. If God was in His heaven, I got on top of the furnace grate in time to brush my teeth."

Jane of St. Anthony Park: "When I was little, my mom would put our towels on the radiator to get them warm while we took a bath. We'd get out, she'd wrap us up in these nice warm towels —and now that I'm over 40, if I'm having a really bad day, sometimes I'll go take a bath, and I'll get my husband to put my towel in the dryer so that it's all nice and warm for me when I get out."

Mongo of Lino Lakes: "My simple pleasure: gettin' up early, five in the mornin', and gettin' out to my fishin' shack, drillin' a couple of holes, settin' up a couple of tip-ups, and goin' inside a nice warm fishhouse and lookin' out the window, sippin' a hot cup of java, and waitin' for them babies to pop up. Can't beat it."

Cubby of Cottage Grove: "On those nights when you're feeling, like, really, really depressed—especially in the wintertime—I have Christmas lights (white ones) around my room, and I turn those on, and I turn on U2's 'One' really, really loud—as loud as my mom will let me have it—and I open the windows so it gets freezing-cold in my room, and I sit there and cry. And that's awesome."

Melissa of Eagan: "My simple pleasure is eating a bowl of Mrs. Fields' chocolate-chip cookie-dough ice cream on a cold winter night, and then taking a very hot bath."

Evil Lynn of White Bear Lake: "When it's really cold outside, one of life's simple pleasures is making microwave popcorn, dumping the popcorn out into the bowl and then squishing the bag with your hands—because the popcorn bag is warm, and your hands are cold, and it makes your hands really nice and toasty-warm after being outside."

Arlene of Inver Grove Heights: "Tonight at my house, it's 28 below zero—which was just what I was waiting for, because my favorite thing to do in the cold, you can't do until [it gets seriously cold] with no wind. And tonight there's no wind, so what

I did is: I grabbed my bottle of children's soap bubbles, and I went outside and blew some bubbles.

"This sounds strange, I know, but bubbles do really neat things when it's this cold. They freeze almost right away—and if, before they freeze, they pop, then little puffs of steam come out. And then after they freeze, you can catch them on your glove or on your bubble-blower, and they just sit there and you can look at 'em—and you can see rainbows in 'em. Sometimes they break into little tiny pieces, or big pieces, and they float down like snowflakes. It's just really cool."

Grandma Up North, in January 1994: "I just wanted to tell you that during our cold, cold freeze—it was about 37 degrees below zero when I remembered—I got out that little jar from October.

"This jar actually does help me remember a beautiful, perfect day. There were butterflies out there in my garden, even in October. I told you guys it would come in handy. Right? I haven't opened it yet. I just look at it and remember how good it was."

The Arizona Penguin of Phoenix: "Hearing about the Minnesota weather while I'm reading the mail at the pool."

Pagan of St. Paul: "My second-floor apartment is very warm and sunny in the winter, and my simple pleasure is walking around naked when the temperature is 25 below zero outside."

Bear of St. Paul: "Spending a long, cold day outside, with the sun beating on me, getting really sweaty—splitting wood all day long, then coming in to a cup of cocoa and sitting by the big fireplace, roasting my feet and enjoying my day's efforts."

Leonard of Shoreview: "I'm sittin' here lookin' out the window at my pond. Have you ever seen a goose land on ice? Pretty graceful."

Another Shirley of Marine: "My simple pleasure is looking out on a Saturday noon at the pond behind my house and seeing three deer slowly sauntering across the snow."

Mandy of Shoreview: "My favorite simple pleasure is hugging a nice warm horse on a cold day. That'll warm you up quicker than anything."

Terri of Greater Minnesota: "I use plastic newspaper bags to pick up doggie doo whenever I walk my dog—an idea I got from Bulletin Board, thank you very much. It's really great on a cold day, when your hands are just freezin', when you pick up that poop and it warms your hand up. It's great."

Sandy of Hudson, Wis.: "I live out in the country, and our doggie just poops all over our yard. I have a metal pooper-scooper—and my favorite, favorite thing is on a cold, cold day when you go out and the poop is frozen. It's so neat and clean; it just pops right into the garbage can, with no problem."

Mary Conroy of Maplewood: "One of my simple pleasures is going out to the van and knocking off those big car turds—you know, the buildup of dirt and salt and snow that piles up behind your tires. It's very satisfying to go out there and just knock one of those off."

Margaret of St. Paul: "I have this old beater car. It's about 13 years old, and it starts all the time in the winter, and it's paid for. The other day, I was kicking one of those big ice chunks off the back of it, and part of my fender fell off with it. And I thought: Boy, that's kinda nice—having a car that's such a beater you don't care if the fender falls off when you kick an ice chunk."

Judy of Inver Grove Heights: "My greatest joy in the wintertime, when it snows: I'm home in my house, surrounded by my husband and kids, and it's snowin' outside, and I don't have to be out there with all the idiots."

Jim J. of St. Paul: "A simple pleasure: driving in the winter, and you pull up to a stop sign, and the defrosters are workin' the snow and ice on the windshield, and right at the top edge of the windshield, all the way around, the snow breaks up and starts to fall down—but you don't use the wipers 'til the exact time when you can sweep away everything! That, to me, is better than sex."

Don of Stillwater: "When you've been lying uncomfortably with the hair dryer on high heat blowing hot air on the frozen water pipes—and the faucet finally starts to drip."

Sailboat Jo of Inver Grove Heights: "A simple pleasure for one who lives not by, but in the Mississippi: It's getting home from work in the evening, trudging to the end of that long, snowy dock, climbing down into the cozy pocket of our sailboat, listening to the bubbler churning the water against the hull and feeling that Arctic breeze rock us around, knowing we're safe and sound.

"A simple displeasure is: on a frigid Minnesota morning, packing my clothes and paraphernalia, hauling it up the ladder and down the dock, driving a block and a half to the nearest shower, and hoping another live-aboard didn't get there first.

"Seems there's a give-up part to everything we get; I guess, the other way around, too."

V.E.M. of Woodbury: "I'm not from Minnesota, and I hate the daggone cold. But when we have these storms and it gets really, really cold and you get that crust on the snow, I just like walkin' out there and crunchin' it. It's just really cool. Almost makes winter worthwhile."

Rita of St. Paul: "Our furnace went down yesterday, and did not work all day. There were icicles hanging off our cat's nose. The furnace man came and fixed it, so today my simple pleasure has been listening to my furnace run. It's wonderful."

Vertically Challenged: "Last summer, I bought a big old mesh hammock at a garage sale, and it was one of the best purchases I ever made. Last fall, on one of those last beautiful, warm days—my birthday—I had my 6-month-old granddaughter out there, and we were layin' in that hammock with her bottle under those beautiful trees—and it was just so peaceful and relaxing.

"And now, when it's so cold and snowy, we can snuggle in a chair and I can remember—and now that spring is getting closer, and the sun feels hotter, I'm really anticipating those warm days when we can put that hammock back up."

Dino of Woodbury: "I was drivin' home from work today, around, oh, 5:30, and I realized that it was still light outside. It was just so wonderful to know that every day, the days are getting just a little bit longer, and spring is gonna be here soon, and nothin' can stop it. So I just wanted to say, 'Hang in there, Bulletin Boarders, 'cause spring is comin'.'"

SIMPLE PLEASURES OF
Solitude

Rosalie of St. Anthony: "I was just noticing, reading people's simple pleasures, that most of them are things that are done alone: skating alone, snuggling into bed alone, getting up and watching the baby alone, driving alone. I'm beginning to think that, really, the greatest simple pleasure is . . . being alone."

E.J. of New Richmond, Wis.: "I have a little baby girl, and my simple pleasure is waking up before she does, and before my alarm goes off, and having time to just sit there with . . . quiet."

Auntie Slick of Spooner, Wis.: "Getting up before the kids and curling up with a trashy novel before chaos erupts."

Middle-aged Mom of North St. Paul: "Getting up in the morning ahead of the rest of the family, sitting at the table with a nice cup of coffee, in my robe and pajamas, and having the Sunday paper all to myself."

Gayle of Lindstrom: "I like it when you wake up really early in the morning and get dressed and take a walk, and then you come back in and slip into bed before everybody else gets up."

Lee of Roseville: "My simple pleasure is playing golf . . . right before dusk. By that time, most players have gone home, the course becomes really quiet and I can play at an unobstructed pace. It's like having the whole place to myself."

Anna of Minneapolis: "I have recently retired, and while other people go to work, early in the morning, I walk six blocks and get the *Pioneer Press* from a little box for 25 cents. I could get it from the drugstore across the street, but where's the pleasure in that? And when I come home again, I sit down, put my feet up and eat a banana while reading the general news. I read the Bulletin Board, and I eat an orange—and then I sip a cup of herb tea and do the crossword puzzle. Now, that is life in the slow lane."

Amy of White Bear Lake: "I just moved out to my own apartment last month, and my simple pleasure is being able to drink out of the milk carton without getting yelled at."

Girl from the Grove: "I'm right now the happiest girl in the whole wide world, because it's 2:41 in the afternoon and I am the only one in my house for the next hour. I just get to sit around and relax, and I don't have to go back to school for musical tonight, and I don't have any homework, and it's just the best, most wonderful simple pleasure in the whole world.

Everyone should try it one day. Highly recommended."

Kelly of St. Paul: "I'm a dog groomer in St. Paul, and during the course of a day, I end up covered with dog hair and feeling pretty grungy—and frazzled; I've been bitten at many times. So my simple pleasure is getting home before the kids, taking a long hot bath, putting on warm sweats and wool socks, curling up on the couch and just listening to the silence."

Raven of Inver Grove Heights: "Life is grand. Here it is, Friday night. I don't have a date, 'cause my husband's at work, but I've got the next-best thing. I'm sittin' on my couch under a nice, big, warm blanket, and I'm watching my all-time favorites: *Planet of the Apes, Beneath the Planet of the Apes* and *Conquest of the Planet of the Apes.* And, on top of it, I'm eating a Dove Bar. And my dog's sittin' next to me, keepin' me company. Boy, life is grand."

Sergeant Bilko of St. Paul: "I don't watch TV, but what I like to do is light a whole lot of candles, a stick of incense, and climb onto bed with lots of pillows and read a mystery. When I'm there, the cats always come and join me, and it's very snug and cozy."

Sir Spam of Cottage Grove: "No. 1: Walking into my bathroom after dark every night and turning the lights way down. Out the window, the sky is the prettiest colors. Some days it's purple/gray/blue; other days, it's yellow/green/gray. It's really neat. No. 2: Playing the piano in a dark house about 2 o'clock in the morning. I can only do this when no one's home, so it doesn't happen that often."

Michelle of St. Paul: "I live with four roommates, so my simple pleasure is when I get to take a shower when no one else is home—because then I can play music in the bathroom and sing really loud in the shower without embarrassment. If you wonder what I sing, it's Whitney Houston's 'Songs from the Bodyguard' CD—so I'm sure it's also my roommates' pleasure not to be here."

Heather of West St. Paul: "I've been house-sitting for my parents since last Friday evening. I've been leaving dishes all over the counter; I didn't take out the trash; I've been leaving my clothes all over the floor; I leave lights on all over, TVs on all over the place, radios; I've been leaving doors open with the air conditioning on—everything that I've waited for 22 years to do, without my mother being here to nag me to pick up after myself and close the doors and shut off the lights and do the dishes and stuff like that. I guess that's my simple pleasure. It's kinda nice just to wallow in the splendor of the mess that I've left behind.

"My parents are coming back Friday, and my other simple pleasure is being able to clean up after myself and look at a nice, spotless house that my mom can be proud to come home to."

BULLETIN BOARD REPLIES: *Your parents' simple pleasure, of course, will be sending you this month's utility bills.*

Hippie Girl of the West Side: "The house is empty, except for my sister; she's asleep, and my dad's at work . . . and my simple pleasure is: You just take a mug full of milk and put it in the microwave for about a minute and a half, so it's nice and hot, stir in about a spoonful of sugar and just sit there sipping your sweet milk. That's a simple pleasure."

Cindy of Rochester: "Simple pleasures: when my husband goes on a business trip, and I can turn up the thermostat to 74 degrees of comfort and then enjoy the silence of three sports channels not being watched simultaneously by the absent channel surfer. It doesn't get much better than this anymore."

Married Man of "somewhere in Ramsey County": "For 14 years—very happily married—I've had to sleep on the left side of the bed, due to kind of an unyielding partner. So the few times a year that I get to travel on business and stay in hotel rooms, I get a queen-size bed and sleep on the right side of the bed. You can kinda spread-eagle all over the bed and just command the whole bed to yourself, without bumping into my lovely wife."

SIMPLE PLEASURES
In Bed

Joan of Shoreview: "My simple pleasure is my bed: a king-size waterbed—heated, of course. It has a nice fluffy mattress pad; then a nice, warm flannel sheet; then a flannel top sheet; then a thermal blanket; then a comforter; then—dah-dah—a down comforter. And my pillow—nice and soft and squishy. All so warm and cozy—and all in a nice pale, pale blue. I love my waterbed; I hate my alarm clock."

John of St. Paul: "I unroll my comforter all the way, start at one side of the bed, and roll up inside it like a cocoon. It is just the coolest, coziest, warmest feeling."

Penny of Cottage Grove (echoed by *Kathy* of Woodbury): "On a cold night, about 15 minutes before going to bed, turn that electric blanket on to '8,' pile some pillows on top of the bed—and when you crawl in, it's really warm."

Anonymous: "While preparing for bed, I open one of those sealed scents that come with department-store statements, place it under my electric blanket and turn up the heat. The aroma soon permeates the room. And so to dream . . . "

Jennifer of Apple Valley: "The most perfectly awesome contentment to me is when you hang your sheets outside after you wash 'em in the summer, and you get that fresh smell, and you get in bed at night and it's perfect."

Tony Mitchell of St. Paul: "Right when you get out of the shower, after you dry yourself off, just jump right into bed in the cool sheets. Simplest pleasure there is—especially on a hot summer night."

Marlene Orth of Maplewood: "My simple pleasure is on a cool, cool fall evening, opening the door in the bedroom and letting the room get really cold—and then I shut it, and my husband and I jump under the covers and warm the bed up. It's a really, really simple pleasure, but it's really fun."

Burger of Cottage Grove: "I'm lying in bed, with my head on the pillow. The pillow gets warm; I can't get to sleep. So I flip it over, and the pillow gets nice and cool, and I can get to sleep."

Millie of St. Paul: "Crawling in bed on a cold night an hour or two after my husband has gone to bed and putting my icy-cold feet up against his nice warm buns. I've been doing this for 30 years, and he just found out about it when I told him I was callin' it in to Bulletin Board."

Kathy of St. Paul: "I love to sleep completely underneath the covers, but I haven't found a partner yet who likes that, too."

Anonymous woman: "Sleeping naked with my cat under the covers, because her fur is soft and warm—and she vibrates when she purrs."

Anonymous woman of St. Paul: "Getting into a cold bed and calling my black Lab up to lie by me, to warm me up. The heat just radiates off his black fur. When I'm nice and toasty, I kick him out—'cause I need a lot of sprawling room. This pleasure is extra-special because I only do it once a week: the night before I change the sheets. He's such a hairy beast, but I love him."

E.H.W. of Oakdale: "After going on vacation and spending a lot of money on a hotel room that's supposed to be really fabulous, but isn't, it's a simple pleasure to come home and crawl into your own bed—clean sheets, comfy pillow, the works. It's heaven."

Bev of Rice Lake, Wis.: "There is absolutely nothing more pleasurable than falling asleep at night in a camping trailer in a quiet campground. The breeze slipping in the window by your bed. The smell of a dying campfire and the muted voices of other campers who are still sitting around their fires talking. A tranquillity overcomes your soul and body that cannot be duplicated."

BULLETIN BOARD REPLIES: *If you're physically capable of it, Bev, try it in a tent, out beside a lake in the wilderness, sometime. See what you think then.*

Honey Bear of Pine City: "My simple pleasure is being able to sleep at night with the windows open, listening to the country night sounds of frogs croaking, owls hooting, and the occasional coyote yipping. I don't hear any cars, only animals."

Annie of Cottage Grove: "A simple pleasure: The first sound of the morning is not the alarm clock; it's the sound of a cooing mourning dove, the calling cardinals and the singing robins. Just a great way to wake up."

Elizabeth of Minneapolis: "My simple pleasure is to set my alarm for the middle of the night—about three in the morning. Then, when the alarm goes off, I wake up and look at the clock—and I think to myself: 'I can go back to bed for four more hours. I'm only halfway through my night's sleep.' It's a great feeling."

Tim of St. Paul: "A simple pleasure: You wake up all sleepy-eyed on a Sunday morning, thinking it's Monday—and then you realize you're wrong. Aaaaaaahhh."

SIMPLE PLEASURES OF
The Road

Bonnie of rural Lindstrom: "A simple pleasure, to me, is driving to work in the morning through the rural countryside—seeing the swan that swims in the pond and just enjoying all there is to see. It's a quiet time for me—my time to get in touch with myself before I begin my day."

The "Cow"girl: "Driving down a country road on a warm spring night with my window rolled down, seeing the farmers working in the fields and smelling the freshly tilled dirt."

Loueeze of Maplewood: "I'm in high school, and I catch a ride with my friends. I've been really, really busy lately, and I hardly ever spend time with my friends anymore, so when there's a big traffic jam, usually everybody hates it, but it's a simple pleasure of mine. When there's a big traffic jam, I get to hang out a little longer with my friends—like maybe five extra minutes on our way to school in the morning."

Anonymous woman of St. Paul: "Tonight I was driving down Kellogg Boulevard, and the Minnesota Orchestra was on MPR playing 'Scheherazade' by Rimsky-Korsakov. It was right at the very end, where it goes 'Daaaah-duh-daaaah-duhduh-daaaam thump-thump.' Anyway, they keep having these thump-thumps, and as you had these big crescendos, I was gliding through intersections just ahead of the red light. Every time I just beat the red light, without trying, you'd have a crescendo in the music. It was really fun."

Bob Woolley of St. Paul: "I really like the Scan and Seek buttons on digital car radios. It saves the drudgery and distraction of knob-fiddling while you're driving, and sometimes you find interesting stations that you'd miss if you stuck to just your old favorites."

Linda of St. Paul: "When we're on long cross-country trips, I like to use Scan and Seek when the station-selector buttons no longer work—to look for little stations in little towns that say things like: 'The F.F.A. at the high school is having a car wash at the Dairy Queen this weekend.' It makes me think that there is someplace on Earth where there are normal people—or else maybe I'm in a time warp for the '50s.

"My son's simple pleasure, in this same circumstance, is when we're coming back home from this long trip, and he pushes the buttons, and one of them responds with one of the local rock stations—so he stops asking us if we're almost home yet. He's so thrilled when he hears it. The power of rock 'n' roll."

Mini Brooke Shields of Highland Park: "Yesterday, we were on an express bus—you know, this great big accordion bus—coming home from Minneapolis. And we were sitting in the accordion part, right in the middle—and we were having such wonderful thrills watching the little circle twist around while the bus turned. It was just so much fun—all that excitement for $1.35!"

Dave of St. Paul: "I was driving home from school today in my Camaro, and I pulled up beside a bus with all these little kids on it, and they all started giving me thumbs-up signs, so I revved up my engine and gave them the thumbs-up, and they all started cheering and giving high-fives to each other. Made me feel really good."

The Interloper of River Falls, Wis.: "I was driving down the highway one time, and I happened to pass by a family of about 20 people who were just about ready to have a picture taken outside, and as I was driving by, I screamed: 'Cheese!' I could see them all start to laugh at once as I drove away. One of the simple pleasures."

Jae of Chetek, Wis.: "One of life's simplest pleasures is driving down the highway and meeting a car in which all the occupants are laughing. Sure puts a smile on my face."

BULLETIN BOARD OBSERVES: *We like it better when everyone except the driver is laughing.*

S.S. of Maplewood: "A simple pleasure: when you come to a four-way stop, and there's another person stopped at the same time, and you're both telling each other to go, and when they do finally go, first they kind of smile or nod their head or they thank you and wave. It's really weird, because you've never seen this person before, and you'll probably never see them again."

Mary of Mendota Heights: "I had a simple pleasure yesterday that is unlikely to be repeated any time soon.

"I was waiting to make a left turn into a parking lot, and there was a guy waiting to make a left turn out of the parking lot—so he couldn't go until I did. He apparently thought I was being overly cautious in waiting for a break in the oncoming traffic, so we were doing the usual irritated signals: He was looking exasperated, and I was sort of shrugging, as if to say: 'What do you want from me?'

"We finally made our turns, at the same time, and as we passed, I figured he'd give me the usual obscene gesture—but instead, we caught each other's eyes and simultaneously started laughing. In this age of such anger and fear, it was nice to—just for a second—be on the same wavelength with a stranger and be able to laugh at ourselves."

Rory of St. Paul: "My simple pleasure is being an amateur, do-it-yourself mechanic, and having an older car that looks beat up—but you have it tuned up so it runs great, as good as a new car—and pulling alongside a new car at a stoplight, and the new car looks great but you hear a really strange noise coming from it that you know you shouldn't be hearing. And you know that your car runs great, even though it looks terrible.

"It's a little sick, and probably malicious, but what can I say?"

Mitch of Eagan: "I work the night shift, and every morning, I drive home at 7 A.M. and watch all the other people goin' to work. Yep, that's my simple pleasure."

Rod of Inver Grove Heights: "The aroma of a new car—before the manufacturer's defects become apparent."

Alice of the West Side: "Sometimes I drive around in cars that need frequent jump starts, and people have helped me a lot by stopping and helping me jump start my car. So I carry around jumper cables.

"The other day, somebody left their lights on, and I was able to help them jump start their car. They didn't have jumper

Simple Pleasures of the Road 101

cables; they didn't know how to use jumper cables; they were stuck out in the middle of a big parking lot. And it just gave me a lot of pleasure to be able to pay back all those people who helped me."

Merlyn of St. Paul: "While driving late at night on unknown roads, it's always comforting to find someone who's going about the same speed as you are, who's just far enough ahead of you that you can follow their taillights and know where the road ahead is going. Having someone to trailblaze for me makes me less anxious about being alone in an unknown place."

Speedy Gonzalez of Oakdale: "Goin' down the road, and you meet a cop, and you look down at your speedometer to realize you're not even goin' the speed limit. There's no better feeling than that one."

Charlie of Eagan: "I just love it when I'm driving down the highway and someone passes me going so fast they almost blow your doors off, and you see them a few miles later, down the road, with a state trooper behind them. I find that very pleasurable. It's justice."

Emmett of Colby, Wis.: "You know, on them sloppy days when we have the big meltdown, my simple pleasure is to let my windshield get all gunked up with the stuff—of course, not enough so I can't see, but close—and then hittin' them windshield washers and cleanin' it all off. It's like a brand-new day dawning before me. Just wonderful. Reminds me of spring."

Bear of St. Paul: "My wife hates to have the windshield dirty. When I drive, I kind of torture her a little bit by letting the windshield get just a little dirtier than it should be. I watch her squirm, put her hands under her seat, and wait and wait—until I finally push the squirter button and let the windshield get cleaned. Then she relaxes and lets out a sigh. That's her simple pleasure."

Annaonymous of Roseville: "Simple pleasures (if you ever had a beater with broken squirters and had to drive around with your window open and a spray bottle of Windex): a really ultra-sloppy day (melting snow, with high concentrations of sand and road salt), and the sun is out, and it's warm enough for the glop to dry quickly when it hits your windshield . . . and your squirters work, and you have plenty of blue juice, and your wiper blades actually make full contact with your windshield."

Bryan of St. Croix Beach: "I went to a gas station the other day, and they actually had those windshield washers with the long handle. Good grief! I didn't have to stretch across my dirty car to reach the other side of the windshield; I could do it all in one swipe with that nice long handle. It was great."

Jenny of St. Paul: "A full tank of gas. I love watching the arrow go from E to F."

L.C. of St. Paul: "Driving in the rain and going under a bridge—and the silence that you hear while you go under the bridge."

Walt of Wayzata: "I just got new tires on my car, and after the big snow, I discovered a simple pleasure: seeing those crisply etched tread marks in the brand-new snow. Well, I told you it was simple. C'mon now; get real."

David Stever of St. Paul: "Remember when you were a kid, and it had just snowed, and there would be piles of snow—not over the top of the car, but just a foot or two tall—in parking lots, and do you remember trying to convince your dad or your mom to drive through the piles of snow? I don't think my mom or dad ever did it; maybe once or twice.

"Well, I'm 40 years old now, and I have a car—and this is gonna sound like one of those stupid Tony the Tiger commercials, but I have to confess that every time I come across a pile of snow in a parking lot, I go out of my way to drive through it.

"By God, I'm gonna teach my kids to do this, too."

Ann of Woodbury: "My simple pleasure is going over a resurfaced road and hearing all the rocks sprinkle up on the bottom of my car."

Teri of Shoreview: "After riding on gravel roads and dirt roads all weekend at the cabin, one of the nicest simple pleasures is riding on a tar road—until, of course, you hit the potholes."

Kathy of West Lakeland: "One of life's simple pleasures is discovering, during a 15-hour road trip from Minnesota to Memphis, that you actually have stopped someplace that has a sparkling-clean, well-taken-care-of rest room. It was such a pleasure to walk into the one and only one that we found during the 15-hour trip."

Sergeant Sue of Apple Valley: "Coming back from a long road trip across the country, 2,000 miles, and finally seeing a sign that says 'Twin Cities.' Maybe it's 300 or 400 miles away, but the first time we see the sign, it's a simple pleasure."

SIMPLE PLEASURES
All Over

Anonymous woman of St. Paul: "One of life's simplest pleasures, but most appreciated, is a good, kind, genuine smile."

Roni of Maplewood: "My simple pleasure is when I'm having a hard day and the only friend I feel I can really count on comes up and gives me a hug without me even saying anything."

G.F. of parts hereabouts: "A new simple pleasure: Went campin' this weekend with my good buddy Tim, who is a prince of a fellow. A man's man. The best guy you'll ever meet. We camped out down at Whitewater; did a little fishin'.

"Last August, I got him turned on to fly-fishing; he's rabid; it's great. I taught him to tie flies—and I'll tell ya: This morning, I was sittin' down trying to put on an even smaller fly than the one I had on. I looked upstream, and there's my dear, dear friend, and he has just hooked and is currently playing a fish—and I get to sit there and know that I taught him to fish, I taught him to tie flies, and he's up there having the time of his life.

"That's epic. I loved it."

A.L. of St. Paul: "These are some of my simple pleasures: going up north with my best friend of 42 years to her lake home for a few days. Oh, the peacefulness of getting away from our families, cooking what we like, reading our favorite books, going for a nice stroll, looking for pretty rocks and hoping to see a few deer. We also like to fish, and we love playing Uno 'til 1 A.M. And the only sound to wake up to in the morning is the singing of the birds. Another favorite thing is walking in the woods in the fall—hunting wild mushrooms, taking them home and cooking them. Boy, what a great smell!"

Troy of St. Paul: "Three of us were just out at Cognac McCarthy's, and we were enjoying some fine Summit Winter Ale and smoking a great Honduran cigar and talking religion— and all of us just stopped and basically said together: You know, this is one of life's little pleasures—a fine drink on a cold night, and the wonderful comfort of two really great friends. That's the true wealth in life."

Carrie of Wisconsin: "My simple pleasure is when you have a pimple, and it's just ready to pop. It's ripe, you know, and you pop it, and it squirts out and hits the mirror. It's the greatest feeling in the world."

The Poet Who Didn't Even Know It of River Falls, Wis.: "A

clear, dark night, to see the stars.

"A frozen chocolate candy bar.

"A candy-apple '60s car.

"A beautiful woman, seen from afar."

Carrie's Evil Twin of St. Cloud: "This may not be a very '90s-woman thing to do—or maybe it is—but having a mostly business meeting with a very attractive man . . . you know, working on that eye-contact thing . . . and sitting there wondering what it would be like to lean right across the desk and kiss him."

Biz of Woodbury: "When I see fresh asphalt just laid, I get all tingly and have to run and get my Rollerblades. It's just an exciting, awesome thing, the virgin asphalt."

Tina of Hastings: "My simple pleasure is sitting, oh, three feet from a recreational fire and watching those glowing sparks dance up into the sky and slowly fade away."

Jack the Carpenter of Minneapolis: "A couple of years ago, on a trip to the Boundary Waters—my wife, my son, our two little dogs—we camped on a high, rocky promontory. Two beautiful bald eagles floated slowly overhead, not more than 30 feet in the air. If you've never seen a bald eagle that close, you've missed a beautiful sight."

Lowell of Cottage Grove: "Checking the nest boxes on my

bluebird trail—and finding four new nests last Fourth of July weekend. A profound simple pleasure: One time I put up a nest box and walked 75 feet back to the car; I turned around, and there was a bluebird sitting on the box."

E.D. of Cumberland, Wis.: "At the bird feeder: seeing the red-bellied woodpecker stand up to the bully blue jay, and seeing the blue jay fly away."

K.D. of St. Paul: "I love it when I swat two flies that are . . . procreating? I just love it."

John of Robbinsdale: "My simple pleasure, one of many—combined with a little touch of malice—is to take the last pennies in the penny cup at the cash register to pay my bill. Sometimes the reverse is also true: When the penny cup is empty and I get some pennies as change, I like to dump them in the cup with a loud clink and walk away feeling like everybody's lauding me for being such a generous soul."

High Up on Iglehart of St. Paul: "When you go through your store coupons and find some that have expired—and you can finally throw those out."

Nancy of Roseville: "When you buy something, and it's on sale, and you didn't expect it to be on sale."

Jennifer of Dellwood: "I go to school down in Iowa, where

there's absolutely nothing comparable to Marshall's or T.J. Maxx. So whenever I come home, I drag my mother especially to T.J. Maxx to go shopping—and this brings me to my simple pleasure, which is the bra bin.

"They have this big table full of bras, all tangled up and twisted together, and you have to dig and hunt and search to find anything. What I really love—what really makes my . . . God, my week!—is when I find a Victoria's Secret bra in my size for a fourth of the price that I'd pay at Victoria's Secret."

Jody of Roseville: "When you try on a swimming suit or a pair of jeans—and it fits like a glove. Best feeling in the world."

Nancy of Lakeville: "Putting on a freshly laundered pair of jeans—and finding money in the pocket."

Debbie of Inver Grove Heights: "I was driving by a golf course, and I saw what looked to be an old, retired man out walking along the fence with a golf club waving in the grass—and there he found an abandoned golf ball. Here's this old guy out picking up stray golf balls, and I suppose he'll give them to his grandchildren or sell 'em at a garage sale. I thought: Well, there's a man that's just had a simple pleasure."

The Red Fox: "When I buy a pack of baseball cards and get a lot of really lame players—and then all of a sudden, I turn up a really good player—like Kirby Puckett or Frank Thomas or Nolan Ryan."

The Butterfly of St. Paul: "Going to the library and finding both books I wanted on the shelf."

Celeste of St. Paul: "The public library. I can go in, and there are just millions of books and tapes and magazines and everything! It's all there, or it can be ordered—and it doesn't cost a cent. Do you know what a miracle that is? If Congress tried to put forth the idea now of starting a public library system, it would never happen."

Charly of St. Paul: "The other night, I actually saw my son using that very expensive set of encyclopedias we bought a few years ago—and are still paying for."

The Music Man of St. Paul: "I just went to look up something about the composer Edouard Lalo in my *Encyclopedia Britannica.* I was looking over the guide words on the spines of the various volumes, to find the right one to pull off the shelf—and lo and behold, there was LALO right there on the spine.

"I think I bought this set in 1974, and this is the first time in almost 20 years that the thing I've wanted to look up has actually been sitting right on the spine—telling me which volume it's in, without having to think about alphabetical order.

That's a pretty rare simple pleasure."

Moose of Concordia College: "The other day, I was writing a paper and preparing for a class, and I had about seven books on the table here—all opened up to the right pages. I've got my desk shaped in an L here, and I've got a rolly chair, and I was just rolling from one leg of the L to the other, and it was fun to have all these books open; it felt kind of . . . scholarly, just poring over all these books."

Sheri of Bemidji: "When you've been working on a really hard calculus problem for a half-hour to 45 minutes, and you finally get an answer, and you look in the back of the book and you actually have the right answer. It doesn't happen too often—but when it does, it's a real pleasure."

The Snackmeister of St. Paul: "Yesterday at a fast-food restaurant, I placed a moderately complicated order. The simple pleasure—almost a simple miracle—is that the young man behind the counter, without taking notes or punching any buttons on the computer, quoted the order back to me perfectly, the first time, without any hesitation.

"To compound the miracle, he rang it up on the computer correctly and charged me the right amount and gave me the right amount of change.

"Of course, what I ordered was not quite exactly what he ended up putting in the bag, as I discovered when I got it home. But you can't ask for everything."

Lenny Bruce of Oakdale: "I recently got a fabulous job, and my simple pleasure is getting the Sunday paper and not having to look in the Jobs section. It's great. I can just skip past that puppy."

Jaybird of Wilson, Wis.: "Right now, it's about 4:25 A.M.; I get in to work about 4 o'clock, before everybody else, and because I get here first, I make the coffee. We've got one of those big 30-gallon coffeepots that accumulates about nine gallons of sludge—and I had one of my greatest simple pleasures this morning: I got to work, and somebody else had cleaned out the coffeepot for me, so all I had to do was put in the water and the coffee. Man, it doesn't get any better than this."

Ken of Coon Rapids: "One of my simple pleasures in life is coming to work and finding that the person who bitches and moans and groans all day is sick and can't come to work that day."

Pat of Roseville: "My simple pleasure is when I get a hole in my nylons in an inconspicuous spot, and it doesn't run all day long. That's wonderful."

A.W. of St. Paul: "My simple pleasure is seeing a little kid who has not yet learned to swear."

Jeannie of Stillwater: "Me and my husband, we have four kids. He has a full-time job and a part-time job, and is also a partner in an antique shop. I have two part-time jobs. And our simple pleasure is to go out of town and stay in a hotel and just lay around at night and watch cable TV. We love the stuff that's on cable TV, but we would never get it in our home—'cause our kids would watch all that crap."

Reid of Roseville: "My simple pleasure is when you go out and buy a tape or CD, and you open the package, and the words are there for you to sing along."

Bethany of St. Paul: "I really enjoy peeling the plastic protective coating off, like, mirrors, VCRs, clocks, that they put on there when they package things."

Hippie Girl of the West Side: "The moment of anticipation when you're standing onstage during a theater performance . . . and you feel the heat of the lights start to come up. That half-second, right there, is the most wonderful feeling—the adrenalin, the happiness, the anxiety, the preparation all come together in that one half-second as the lights rise. It's beautiful; it's a beautiful thing."

Kacie of Sunfish Lake: "I'm a pianist, and one of my greatest simple pleasures is sitting down at the piano with my new song in front of me and being able to play it from beginning to end without any major screw-ups."

Curly Top of Le Sueur: "Getting off the roller coaster—that wonderful feeling that you've survived, that you're still alive. What a feeling."

Ginny Johnson of Roseville: "My simple pleasure is to go into my favorite beauty shop looking like Clarabelle the Clown and to come out looking like Cindy Crawford—at least from the forehead up."

Dr. Ogre: "A simple pleasure: a good face shot in the paper—kinda big, so you can draw a bunch of stuff on it, like missing teeth and a goatee, maybe a couple of real thick eyebrows (those work best for the ladies), a new set of eyes, etc., etc."

Louisa of St. Paul: "I jumped on the scale this morning and realize that I'm within 10 pounds of what my driver's license says. How's that for a simple pleasure?"

Kathy of St. Paul: "I'm an avid workoutaholic. I either jog or ride an exercycle or go to the club—nearly every day. And a simple pleasure—an extremely simple pleasure—is granting myself a night off from working out when I never expected it.

"I get home, and maybe I'm lookin' at the snow and playing

with my dogs—and decide: It's just the right night to take a night off; I'll hit it hard tomorrow night. It's wonderful."

The Crayola Queen, in a 2:15 A.M. call: "My simple pleasure is when I'm working late at night—and this is especially great after a long day like today—and there's no one else even awake, and being so tired that I could just lay down and fall asleep right on the floor. And then all of a sudden, this huge burst of energy just comes and makes me wanna, like, dance on the tables with bells on my toes, singin' at the top of my lungs. It's really groovy; I like it a lot."

Bob Woolley of St. Paul: "The deadbolt lock on my front door has been getting stickier and stickier. Finally, I got so fed up with it that I went down to the store and bought a little squirt can of WD-40. I was amazed. One little spritz in there, and the deadbolt worked better than I've never known it to work—even when it was new.

"So, simple pleasure No. 1 is having a lock on the front door that works without any effort and without any fuss. And simple pleasure No. 2 is to discover that there's actually one product on the market that works as well as its ads claim."

Red's Daughter of Hastings: "My simple pleasure is when a young man opens a door for you and shows a little respect."

Dan of Cottage Grove: "It's nice to walk out to the mailbox, and, when you sort through your mail, you find out that you have more checks coming to you than bills. Kinda neat."

Molly of Mac-Groveland: "Sending off the last payment on a bill. I just get this warm, fuzzy feeling when I send it off in the mail, knowing that I'm never, ever going to see that bill in my mail again."

Mean Mark of White Bear Lake: "My simple pleasure is to see the people who overextended themselves in the '80s filing Chapter 13 now."

Anonymous couple of Baldwin, Wis.: "Our simple pleasure: when our loud-talking, boring neighbor at the lake, who spends most of our waking hours at our place, leaves at 8:30 P.M. announcing 'See you tomorrow' rather than 'See you in a little while'—returning by 9 or 9:30, as a rule."

Sir Spam of Cottage Grove: "I found a simple pleasure when I went to the dentist a couple of days ago. It is a really great feeling when they squirt the water in your mouth with that little gun—especially when they just brushed your teeth with the gritty toothpaste."

Keith of Dayton: "I have a simple pleasure: getting a brand-new toothbrush, with nice stiff bristles. They clean your teeth so nice, after having one that's been all bent and flattened out."

Loueeze of Maplewood: "I just got a brand-new asthma inhaler, and it's really awesome. It's great having a new inhaler, because when I had attacks and I used my old one, there was like nothing left in it, so it took a long time for it to kick in, you know? But now, with a brand-new inhaler, it's just really potent and it works so fast and good. Really cool."

J.D. of Red Wing: "My simple pleasures are brushing my teeth and sneezing—of course, not at the same time. I'm always stuffed up, so one teensy-weensy moment of clear breathing is heavenly. But you can only take so many decongestants and antihistamines, so I love to sneeze."

Joe of Spring Valley, Wis.: "I grew up on a dairy farm in the '50s.

"My first pleasure has to do with farming in the summer. One of the things you do all summer is mow hay, and anybody who's ever done it will never forget it. It's hot, dusty, miserable work. At the end of the day, your nose is full of incredible hay-flavored green boogers—but slowly, through the summer, you fill up the haymow.

"By September, hopefully, it's a little cooler, and you're putting your last cutting of hay in the barn. With any luck, you're right up to the rafters. You finally get the last bale off the last load in that barn, and you lay down and smell all that green hay, and you think: 'Hey, we're ready for winter. Let 'er rip.'

"My second simple pleasure has to do with winter. If you've ever been in a dairy barn in the winter at milking time, you know it's an incredibly peaceful place. It's quiet; all you hear are cows chewing their cuds, a little clinking of their stanchions. Outside, it can be howling-cold, but all those warm bodies give off a lot of heat.

"I can remember, every morning and every night, going up to the barn, hand-milking our 14 Guernsey cows. You'd sit there and milk with your brothers, and after a while, you'd get bored and start squirting the cats, who were pretty appreciative. And after you got tired of squirting the cats, you'd start squirting your brothers. A Super Soaker's got nothing on a Guernsey cow—either in volume or in range. We'd blast each other with milk—and hopefully, my father wouldn't come along and catch us and give us hell.

"Even though it does, yes, smell a little bad, a dairy farm's a pretty pleasant place."

Farmer Mom of Wilson, Wis.: "My elder daughter, Soupy, came inside after cleaning out the cows' stalls and announced that her simple pleasure is realizing that she did not have to muck out the Ark."

G.F. of parts hereabouts, with "a simple pleasure that started out as a gripe (the best ones do):

"I live in an apartment, and when I have stuff in the dryer, it gets done and the next person to come through pulls my stuff out of the dryer, wads it on top of the machine, wedges it back in there in a corner next to the coin-accepter slot—and when I come down, I've got a pile of ironing to deal with. I hate it—so . . .

"I learned a long time ago: Lead by example. When I come through and I have to pull somebody else's stuff out of the dryer, I take their stuff out and fold it! It takes me five minutes; it makes their day; everybody's happier.

"The last time I did this, the owner of the clothing happened to be female; I could tell because I ended up folding a skirt. [BULLETIN BOARD NOTES: *It's a good guess, anyway.*] When I went down there to pick up my own stuff, there was just a little quick note on the dryer, saying 'Thank you!'—and a little bag of heart candy, which I thought was really swell.

"Just a little acknowledgment of a nice thing really made my day."

Kathy of St. Paul: "A simple pleasure: buying $20 or $30 or $40 worth of food for the food shelves—whatever it is I've budgeted; usually it ends up more—and then, on top of it, adding things for kids, like cookie-decorating sugar for Christmas cookies, and animal crackers—that kind of thing."

Marlis of St. Paul: "Throwing out a bag of bread crumbs, and watching all the birds and squirrels eating."

Anonymous woman of Minneapolis: "I hope this doesn't sound completely smug, but I'll take a chance. I really feel a simple pleasure when I get that nice lightheaded feeling after giving a pint of blood—which is free, and they give you cookies afterward, and it makes me feel like maybe I've contributed something."

The Nightingale: "About five years ago, I was at the doctor's office, having my eyes examined. While I was waiting with the drops in my eyes, a small boy of about 5 years of age was looking at me. He had a cast on one leg, and crutches. He was printing on a piece of paper.

"Soon he came over to me and handed me the paper. He had printed: 'I think you are pretty.' Boy, did he make my day. I'm now 83 years of age.

"Bless you, little boy."

Retired Al of the East Side: "I go out to Maplewood Mall, to Circus Pizza, and play these crane machines. My simple pleasure is when I'm standing pulling out a toy or a prize, and there's a little child next to me just dancing with excitement to see me win something.

"But the biggest pleasure is to see the look on their face when you hand 'em that toy and say: 'Here. It's yours.'"

Lindsay of North Oaks: "One of life's simplest pleasures is sitting at home in a comfortable chair, reading everyone else's simplest pleasures."